Strategic Planning

for

Information Systems

Revised Edition

Strategic Planning
for
Information Systems

Revised Edition

Written by
Robert V. Head

Foreword by
James C. Emery

Q.E.D. Information Sciences, Inc.
Wellesley, Massachusetts 02181–0501

STRATEGIC PLANNING FOR INFORMATION SYSTEMS

Printed in the United States of America

First edition: 1979

First revised edition: March, 1982

Library of Congress Catalog Card Number: 82-80713

International Standard Book Number: 0-89435-054-4

To Robert and Colleen

Contents

CHAPTER 1 BASIC CONSIDERATIONS IN SYSTEMS PLANNING 1

  1.1   WHAT IS STRATEGIC INFORMATION SYSTEMS PLANNING? 4

  1.2   ORIGINS OF SYSTEMS PLANNING 10

  1.3   ELEMENTS IN SYSTEMS PLANNING 14

  1.4   CONCEPTUAL ASPECTS OF PLANNING 20

  1.5   UNCERTAINTY IN PLANNING 27

  1.6   IS STRATEGIC PLANNING REALLY NECESSARY? 32

  1.7   BENEFITS OF PLANNING 34

CHAPTER 2 THE ORGANIZATIONAL ENVIRONMENT 39

  2.1   SCOPE OF SYSTEM PLANNING 42

  2.2   INFORMATION RESOURCES MANAGEMENT 43

  2.3   SYSTEMS PLANNING AND CORPORATE PLANNING 45

  2.4   SYSTEMS PLANNING AND BUDGETING 49

  2.5   SYSTEMS PLANNING AND PROJECT PLANNING 51

  2.6   LEVELS OF PLANNING 59

  2.7   PLANNING IN A DECENTRALIZED ENVIRONMENT 63

  2.8   CONVERSION PLANNING 64

CHAPTER 3 THE METHODOLOGY OF SYSTEMS PLANNING 71

  3.1   INVOLVING TOP MANAGEMENT 72

  3.2   ORGANIZING FOR PLANNING 72

  3.3   DATA COLLECTION 77

  3.4   MANAGERIAL AND USER REQUIREMENTS 87

  3.5   PROJECTING DEMAND FOR SERVICES 91

  3.6   TECHNOLOGY ASSESSMENT 93

  3.7   EPISODIC VERSUS ANNUALIZED PLANNING 96

CHAPTER 4 PRACTICALITIES IN SYSTEMS PLANNING 101

  4.1   DETERRENTS TO EFFECTIVE PLANNING 101

  4.2   CONTROL MECHANISMS 104

  4.3   SCOPE AND FORMAT OF PLANS 111

  4.4   GUIDELINES FOR PLANNING 119

APPENDIX: ASSESSING SYSTEMS PLANNING EFFECTIVENESS 123

INDEX 175

List of Figures

1-1 Evolution of Data Processing Technology 2

1-2 Objective Statement 7

1-3 Goals, Objectives and Projects 9

1-4 Advanced Planning Framework 22

1-5 Levels of Data Usage 24

1-6 Systems Planning Projection 29

1-7 Systems Planning Possibilities 30

1-8 Systems Planning Profile 31

2-1 Stages of DP Growth 40

2-2 Business Planning and Systems Planning 47

2-3 The Resource Allocation Problem 52

2-4 Priority Criteria for New Systems Initiatives 54

2-5 Project Life Cycle 58

2-6 Key Activities of the Initiation Phase 60

2-7 Levels of Systems Planning 61

2-8 Software Conversion Prioritization 66

3-1 Equipment Inventory Data Elements 79

3-2 Distribution of Computer Resources 80

3-3 Application Inventory Data Elements 81

3-4 Assessment of Current Applications 82

3-5 Analysis of Ongoing Projects 83

3-6 Personnel Summary 84

3-7 Current and Projected Costs 86

3-8 Application Planning Form 90

3-9 Workload Projection 92

3-10 Cross Impact Matrix 97

4-1 Outline of Systems Plan 112

4-2 Major Oil Company Ten Year Plan 114

4-3 Military Agency Master Plan 115

4-4 Federal Agency Ten Year Plan 116

4-5 State Government Three Year Plan 117

4-6 Finance Company Three Year Plan 118

Foreword

Most organizations seem to exhibit a bias against planning. Planning is, after all, contemplative and cerebral -- and maybe even a little sissy. A he-man wants to get on with the job, perhaps adding to the surprise and excitement by not adhering to any well-plotted course.

Planning suffers from the fact that it deals with a distant and uncertain future: any benefit comes later, and may be reaped long after the incumbent planner has left the scene. Solving the latest short-term crisis -- or failing to solve it -- has immediate consequences that drive out, in Gresham-like fashion, considerations of more distant effects. Furthermore, it has not helped the cause for planning that it has often been done more as a ritual than an operational tool. Too many plans end up on forgotten shelves.

We pay a heavy price for failure to plan adequately. A considerable fraction of the less successful information systems undoubtedly suffer from poor planning and follow-up. Problems of mismatch between information needs and system capabilities will not be eliminated by the best of planning, but good planning will certainly mitigate the consequences of changes in the technology, the environment and the organization itself.

Sensible planning has to be as concerned with its own cost-effectiveness as it is concerned with the cost-effectiveness of an information system. This means that the expected benefits of planning must be balanced against its cost. In some cases this may call for planning in excruciating detail, while in others a quick back-of-the envelope analysis may suffice. An experienced planner understands this, and avoids planning for its own sake.

Robert Head's book does not lay down step-by-step procedures for infallible planning. Rather, it provides a rationale and a set of concepts for planning. In my experience, it is much more important to approach the task of planning with the right concepts than it is to have an extensive portfolio of techniques. Few authors are as well equipped as Robert Head to argue the case for planning and to point the way in the right direction.

The book is just the right length for my taste: long enough to get the essential message across, and not so long as to bog down in unnecessary details. It can be read comfortably in a few pleasant hours. An information systems professional should certainly be willing to devote this level of effort to gain sound insights about systems planning and how it can be made more effective.

James C. Emery

Preface to the Second Edition

Two related phenomena within the information systems community have served in recent years to underscore the importance of doing a better job of planning for future systems.

First, almost all organizations -- whether large or small, commercial or public-service -- have witnessed a continuing increase in the demand for resources allocated to information processing. This signifies more than merely additional dollars budgeted for personnel, equipment and software; it suggests, more significantly, that automated information systems are intruding further and further into the mainstream of the organization's operations and indeed into the process of managerial decision making itself. No longer is the province of information systems restricted to traditional transaction processing applications such as invoicing or payroll; it now comprehends other more complex and potentially more costly application areas.

Accompanying this growth in the scope and importance of information systems has been a heightened concern on the part of top management with the effective usage of systems technology. This is no doubt due in part to the swelling demand for additional resources for information systems, but that is only part of the picture. There is also growing understanding on the part of management of the true potential of systems technology and the contribution it can make to the attainment of organizational objectives. Today, as a new generation of managers ascends within the company hierarchy, more and more chief executives can be found who have an educational and professional background imbued with systems concepts and a managerial style that is compatible with quantitative methods.

Given this newly emergent organizational climate, it has become evident that better systems planning is needed. In the negative sense, such planning helps assure that resources will be applied in the future in a near optimal manner and that systems development fiascos of the kind that have plagued many organizations in the past will be avoided. In a more positive vein, planning helps select systems projects that offer the greatest future benefits to managers and other users -- projects that extend the role of computer based systems into vital facets of both policy level and operational management.

As I have tried to suggest, getting started to produce an information systems plan isn't easy. Many aspects of such planning require not only hard work but an innovative attitude on the part of both planners and top management. Where there is an established pattern of formalized strategic planning for the organization as a whole, the task of systems planning becomes easier, but it still requires specialized procedures of its own.

What I offer here is not a "techniques" book on systems planning but rather one that seeks to enunciate first principles, provide an overview of planning methodology and identify problems likely to be encountered. Though Chapter 3, on methodology, has been greatly expanded in the second edition, it remains doubtful whether the planning novice will ever be able to find a proven set of methods and procedures that can simply be put in place within his particular organizational milieu.

Surveys indicate that almost all large organizations with data processing budgets in the tens of millions of dollars annually now are committed to some form of information systems planning, but there is wide diversity in the effectiveness and quality of these plans. For this reason, there are few models to cite and few planning processes that their originators would dare advance as "ideal" approaches.

Because the initiation and conduct of systems planning is an important managerial responsibility, I am hopeful that this work will, first of all, be meaningful to managers responsible for overall strategy and, second, to information systems managers directly responsible for effective usage of systems resources. Computer professionals concerned with planning should also find the discussions of interest and perhaps find points of departure for particularizing planning concepts within their own working environment. Finally, students of management may gain an acquaintance with planning practices that are being increasingly applied both by business managers and public administrators.

Much of the material presented here was developed for workshops sponsored initially by the Society for Management Information Systems and subsequently by the Washington Chapter of the Data Processing Management Association. I am grateful to the organizers of these sessions for stimulating me to try to put together a cohesive overview of this subject matter.

Since the first edition of this book was published in 1979, I have accumulated a wealth of additional material on strategic planning, some contributed by participants in my seminars and workshops and some derived from my own research efforts. The original work has been augmented with additional textual material in chapters one, two and three, with a substantial number of new figures accompanying every chapter and with the addition of an appendix on assessment of information systems planning efforts.

Robert V. Head
Washington, D.C.
November 1981

Chapter 1
Basic Considerations in Systems Planning

"I hold that man is in the
right who is most closely
in league with the future."
                    -- Henrick Ibsen

There is much evidence to suggest that changes are impacting our society with more rapidity than ever in the past and that the *rate* of change is itself accelerating. This rapidity of change affects, of course, all individuals and institutions.

An illustration of the rapidity of change in information systems can be drawn from the development of business machines as illustrated in Figure 1-1. It took roughly eighty years for the key-driven desk calculator to evolve from its crude mechanical beginnings before the turn of the century into the streamlined solid state device we use today. it took only forty years, though, for punched card tabulating equipment to advance from the first pioneering installations of the thirties. It took just twenty years for the first general-purpose computers, developed out of the discoveries of World War II, to reach an impressive threshold of fast and reliable operation by the mid-sixties. Another major breakthrough -- communication-based on-line systems -- reached maturity in less than ten years. And today's most significant technological innovation -- the minicomputer -- has come to fruition within five short years.

What implications does this increase in the velocity of systems change hold for systems management?

In the past, those responsible for the systems function in an organization could, with some confidence, look several years into the future and not envision substantial change in the methodology of their activity. The advent of the electronic computer dealt the first rude blow to the comfortable feeling that, in the systems realm as elsewhere in the business, things were likely to be much the same in the

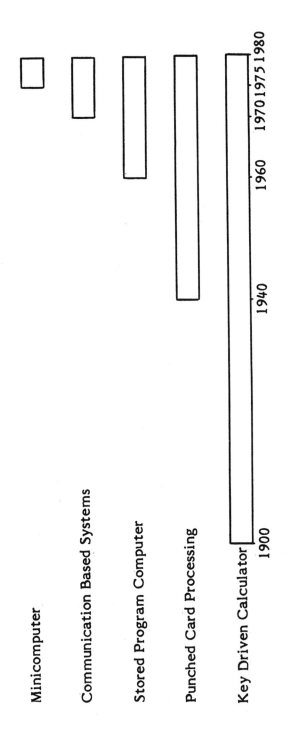

Figure 1-1/Evolution of Data Processing Technology

future as they had been in the past. Today, with a proliferation in the techniques and tools of information systems an undeniable reality, those managers not capable of introducing a more disciplined planning approach into their area of responsibility will be ill-prepared to cope with the rapidly changing era that lies ahead.

The idea of strategic planning for information systems has gained adherence within the recent past, to the point where systems people in both government and industry are conducting at least rudimentary efforts at such planning. For many reasons, which we will explore later, the quality of this strategic planning varies widely. In some instances, application project plans or projections of equipment capacity requirements are labelled as "strategic" plans. In others, planning goals are so broadly stated that they bear little relevance to the practical problems of systems management.

Despite the growing maturation of information processing, and the heightened interest in strategic planning, there is as yet little recognition of systems planning as a discipline or major subdiscipline within the professional community of computer managers and specialists. There is also a dearth of literature devoted to information systems planning, and what is available does not reveal a real consensus as to the nature and scope of this form of planning activity.

We can expect that, as more organizations broaden their acquaintance with the practicalities of planning and as more contributions to the theory and methodology appear, systems planning and those who engage in it will gain greater recognition within the professional and business communities. Two avenues of progression will undoubtedly go hand in hand. As more organizations decide that it is worthwhile -- even vital -- to devote resources to systems planning, they will provide a stimulus to conceptual and methodological advances by academicians, consultants and others concerned with improving business systems. These contributions to the theory of systems planning will in turn encourage more effective applications.

This has happened over the past twenty-five years or so in the broader field of corporate planning. As both theory and practice have advanced, a new literature has emerged, accompanied by sophisticated new tools such as technological forecasting, to aid those concerned with demarcating the future direction of their organizations over an extended period.

1.1 WHAT IS STRATEGIC INFORMATION SYSTEMS PLANNING?

The term "strategic planning" is gaining currency among systems managers as they become increasingly concerned with more formalized and disciplined approaches to identifying requirements beyond the immediate future. The complexity of today's information systems, and the increasingly large share of company resources earmarked to support them, underscore the need for a more carefully prepared "road map" to the future. This is especially so because of the long lead times that typify many of today's large systems projects.

The word "planning" in the context of this discussion connotes a process for *exercising favorable influence* over future events. It is an active rather than a passive exercise, as contrasted to forecasting which is concerned with estimating the future rather than influencing it through actions and decisions.

The word "strategy" has been borrowed from military parlance to convey the notion of an important and high-level form of activity, such as might be required to command a military theater of operations.

STRATEGIC AND TACTICAL PLANNING

As adapted from the military vocabulary, strategic planning has to do with the overall conduct of large-scale operations. This is in contrast to tactical planning, which concentrates on the immediate problems of maneuvering military units in the field to achieve specific objectives. In a business organization, strategic planning reflects the concern of top management with the future direction, profitability, product line and position in the community of the firm, while tactical planning addresses the conduct of day-to-day operations such as getting this week's, or this month's or this year's, workload processed in the form of payroll checks produced, customer accounts updated or airline reservations booked.

Strategic planning for information systems seeks to assure that the organization will be in a position to take full advantage of emerging equipment and software technology to satisfy requirements throughout the planning period. At the tactical level, management must make certain that enough resources are available to support the near term data processing requirements of the organization as, for example, in assuring that an increase in reservations workload can be handled by an airline system or that a growth in account activity can be accommodated by a bank's computers.

Regardless of terminology, most organizations have come to recognize that planning is necessary on these two levels: the tactical, to assure that there is sufficient equipment capacity, along with personnel and other resources, to continue to get the recurring work done; and the strategic, to anticipate what future workloads, and workload processing systems, are likely to be.

LONG-RANGE AND SHORT-RANGE PLANNING

Strategic planning has, by its nature, a long-range rather than a short-range connotation. Though there can be decisions within the near term that have strategic implications, strategic planning tends to cover a time horizon of at least five years into the future, with eight to ten year planning cycles not uncommon. Some organizations segment their plans according to the time scale covered, with strategic planning extending five years and beyond, accompanied by more detailed intermediate level planning two to five years into the future and short-range operating plans encompassing the current year or sometimes the current year plus one.

Though it is certainly desirable to have strategic plans covering a long-range period which provide a framework for guiding and constraining intermediate and short-range planning, experience varies on whether it is preferable to begin with a long-range plan and work backward or to gradually expand short-range planning forward as results are achieved and planning techniques become better understood. In some cases, initial long-range planning efforts have been abandoned as too general and ineffective in favor of concentrating planning resources on near-term problems.

GOALS AND OBJECTIVES

Because information systems planning is concerned with long-range activities, it concentrates on the broad goals an organization is trying to achieve, leaving more specific objectives to be articulated through subordinate planning exercises. A distinction between goals and objectives is useful in delineating the realm of strategic planning.

Characteristically, goals are *enduring statements of purpose*, often not attainable in the short run. They are nonquantitative in nature, not referencing specific resources required for implementation or specific timetables for realization. They are concerned with the fulfillment of broad organizational needs, the achievement of desired levels of performance or the alleviation of major problems.

In the strategic planning milieu, goals can be thought of as general statements indicating the basic direction the organization is seeking to take, as suggested by the following examples:

1. Provide the telecommunications capability to deliver data to any company computer center from any remote site at reasonable cost.

2. Increase the ability to respond to top management requirements for information and facilitate the collection and maintenance of such information.

Characteristically, objectives are subordinated to goals, are narrower in scope and shorter range in nature, and have a reasonable possibility of attainment within specified time periods and levels of resources. Goal statements are the expressions from which objectives are derived. Objectives differ from goals in that they are statements of results to be achieved within a given period. Thus, they have associated with them target dates or milestones for accomplishment and an identification of resource requirements necessary to their achievement. Because objectives are more specific than goals, they can be reflected in the current year budget. An example of an objective statement is shown in Figure 1-2. (See Reference 1 at the end of this chapter.)

1. <u>Objective:</u> Evaluate current and upcoming minicomputer equipment and software capabilities, develop guidelines as to the types of applications for which the mini is technically feasible and cost effective and evaluate potential costs and benefits of distributed processing systems.

   Start date: January 20, 1981

   Completion date: November 30, 1981

2. <u>Background:</u> With the growth of minicomputer capabilities and the decrease in hardware costs, it is increasingly important to develop policy and guidelines for evaluating their use both as network components and as stand-alone systems.

3. <u>Principal Milestones:</u>

   a. Perform a technical review of minicomputer equipment and software capabilities.   March 26, 1981

   b. Survey existing minicomputer and distributed processing installations.   June 28, 1981

   c. Draft of policy and guidelines.   October 15, 1981

4. <u>Resource Estimates:</u>

	12 Month
Mandays (Internal)	180
Mandays (Support)	0
Manday Cost	$16,500
Computer Support	0
Contractual Support	25,000
Other Costs	1,000
TOTAL COST	$42,500
TOTAL MANDAYS	180

5. <u>Constraints:</u> Schedule and plans depend on approval of consultant support.

Figure 1-2/Objective Statement

The strategic information systems plan embodies goals that must be translated into actuality by further defined planning objectives and, at a still lower level of specificity, by project plans. Generally, there should be relatively few goals to be pursued by the organization, perhaps no more than a dozen or so. These might expand into a larger number of subordinate objectives which in turn could generate numerous projects and other activities. This is suggested schematically by Figure 1-3.

Depending on the nature of the goal, there may be a one-for-one correspondence between goals, objectives and projects, as illustrated on the left side of the figure. More typically there will be a variety of planning subactivities engendered by strategic planning goals as suggested at the right hand side of the schematic.

PLANS AND THE PLANNING PROCESS

A distinction should be made between the information systems planning document itself and the process involved in producing it. Some form of strategic planning takes place in almost every organization, but it may not result in a cohesive document that can be described as a system plan. An informal planning process may produce documents such as memoranda, reports and technical notes which in combination approximate a strategic plan.

A comprehensive strategic plan is usually the product of well thought out planning procedures which specify the format of the plan, the schedule for its preparation and the review and approval steps required for its issuance. Sometimes these procedures are extensions or adaptations or procedures that guide all elements of the organization in preparing inputs to corporate plans.

It is, of course, possible to prepare a strategic plan without a set of procedures that spell out the planning process. This sometimes happens as the end product of a task force or other ad hoc effort to put together a plan.

Regardless of the degree of formality in the procedures for performing planning and preparing the planning document itself, the difference between the process of planning and the plan itself should be kept in mind. Information systems

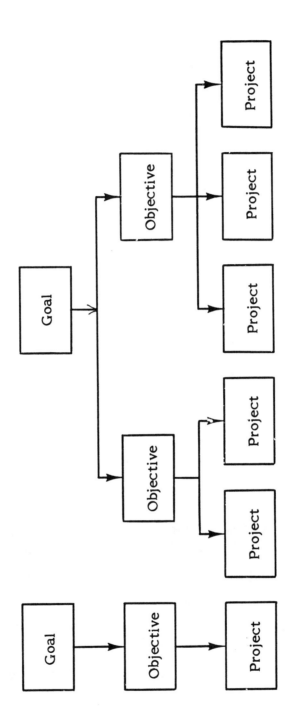

Figure 1-3/Goals, Objectives and Projects

specialists who are assigned the responsibility for preparing a strategic plan must necessarily be concerned with the methodology of planning. Top managers, who must review the plan and make decisions on the allocation of resources to attain planning goals, will be more interested in the content of the plan than in the process used to derive it.

1.2 ORIGINS OF SYSTEMS PLANNING

Though the field of systems planning is relatively new, having gained widespread acceptance even within large companies only in the late 1970's, many of the methods that it utilizes are well established and have been available to planners for some time. Business systems planners have been able to borrow techniques from related kinds of planning, in many instances adapting them to the more specialized and technical milieu of computer systems.

Let us consider briefly the antecedents of systems planning from which the body of techniques that constitute the "tools of the trade" of systems planning have been derived.

BUSINESS PLANNING

Over the past twenty-five years, most large well-managed organizations have adopted formalized approaches to long-range business planning. This emphasis within leading corporations has been accompanied by a growth in business planning literature which has helped to establish the concepts of business planning, the methodology associated with such planning and descriptions of the results of the planning process in particular companies and industries.

Today, practitioners of systems planning will find themselves in one of three environments with respect to business planning:

1. Companies in which there is a set of policies and procedures governing the preparation of business plans. In such situations, the systems plan is either a component part of the business plan or a subordinate document which is cross-referenced or otherwise related to the business plan. The goals and objectives

spelled out for the company as a whole in the business plan engender the formulation of an equivalent set of systems goals and objectives that are agreed upon as being supportive of the overall business plan.

2. Companies in which business goals and objectives are not documented or published for general distribution. In this situation, the systems plan can still be reflective of company goals and objectives if those responsible for systems planning can be made privy to the policies, goals and strategies known to the top management group.

3. Companies in which there is no formalized business planning of any kind. Here, systems planners can still proceed to produce goals and objectives for their area of responsibility, carefully documenting assumptions about what might be a reasonable set of corporate policies, goals and objectives. Once documented, these assumptions can be presented to top management and guidance solicited as to whether they are indeed consistent with top management's thinking, even though this thinking has not been formally documented. This is often referred to as the "bottom up" approach to planning.

With a history of twenty-five years of corporate planning and little more than five years of systems planning in most organizations, the number of cases corresponding to that desribed in the first category above is constantly growing. Hence, business planners and systems planners are coming increasingly to share a methodology first developed and applied within the broader realm of corporate goal setting.

What are these business planning techniques? Many represent an extension of accounting and statistical methods that have been used in forecasting financial and sales performance; others embody more sophisticated modeling techniques in which a variety of external environmental factors, such as government policy, labor demands, consumer buying proclivities, sources of capital investment and other variables are considered. Not all these business planning methods are applicable to the more specialized area of systems planning but, as we shall see, many of them do have their counterpart in the systems planning process.

PROJECT PLANNING

Experience in developing large-scale computer applications during the sixties led to the development and refinement of a substantial body of practices and methods known generally as project planning and control systems. As computer projects grew larger and more ambitious, results were often disappointing in terms of missed schedule dates, cost overruns and failure of systems to meet design objectives and performance requirements. This led to the introduction of project planning and control mechanisms, some of these mechanisms themselves computerized, that permit project managers to make better estimates of project costs and schedules and to maintain closer control of the performance of project teams assigned to implement these schedules.

Among the "classical" and still widely used techniques of project management are the CPM (Critical Path Method) and PERT (Program Evaluation and Review Technique) networking approaches in which estimates are derived for the various activities associated with a project and the events which these activities result in. The "critical path" through such networks gives management insight into which sets of project activities are most vulnerable to delays and cost overruns. Some of these networking techniques for large scale systems projects are horrendously complex, involving sequences of hundreds of activities which must be accomplished before overall project targets can be attained.

Networking techniques are but one of many project planning and control methods that have proven beneficial. Others involve the application of structured analytical and programming approaches, matrix management organizational approaches and life cycle management principles to computer application development projects.

CAPACITY PLANNING

Data processing managers concerned with assuring that their installations will have sufficient processing and storage capacity for future application growth have developed a variety of measuring and forecasting procedures that have come to be characterized generally as capacity planning. Most modern computer installations generate a substantial amount of useful quantitative data as a by-product of normal processing operations. Some of this is used as input to computer performance evaluation activities in which the percentage of utilization of various pieces of equipment can be analyzed and "balanced." Other byproduct data is used as the basis for unit costing, so that the cost per transaction processed or record updated can be identified for each application and, in many cases, used as the basis for a "charging back" user departments served by the data processing installation.

As these measures have been perfected and applied, a history of capacity utilization within the DP installation has been accumulated and made the basis for projections of future demand for computer usage. Though, as we shall see, there are some drawbacks to undue reliance on these projections, they can provide useful insight to systems planners as to when major equipment upgrades can be anticipated throughout the duration of the systems plan.

TECHNOLOGY ASSESSMENT

Out of the complex requirements of the military establishment, and the efforts of "think tank" research organizations dedicated to supporting defense planning, have come a body of techniques directed toward determining the likelihood of future technological occurrences. The methodology of technology assessment is geared to taking an intensive look at technological phenomena that are likely -- or unlikely -- to occur over an extended timeframe, often ten to twenty years. This gives the sponsors of research and development in the technology, and potential users of the technology, a basis for formulating more realistic strategic plans based on such technology.

Technology assessment had its inception more than a quarter century ago in military planning and has since been widely adopted as a planning tool by civil agencies and business organizations. Numerous technology assessments have been undertaken that focus exclusively on computer technology. We shall subsequently discuss technology assessment in more detail.

MANAGEMENT BY OBJECTIVES

In addition to the methodologies just mentioned, systems planning draws heavily upon the body of concepts and techniques that have come to be known as "Management by Objectives" (MBO). The MBO approach has gained acceptance in both government and industry as a planning vehicle for all aspects of organizational activity.

MBO deals with the formulation of goals and objectives and makes careful distinctions between the two in developing and documenting plans.

Thus, it can be seen that information systems planning is really a hybrid as well as a derivative methodology, having its roots in a variety of earlier planning techniques, some originating within and some outside the computer field.

1.3 ELEMENTS IN SYSTEMS PLANNING

The information systems planner must take into account three basic questions in formulating strategic plans:

1.   What is the technology going to be like over the planning period?

2.   What changes will take place in the environment in which the organization must operate?

3.   What are the organization's long-range goals and policies?

These are essentially the same questions that confront top management seeking to formulate overall corporate strategy. In the context of systems planning, they must be particularized to apply to that area of activity. For example, corporate strategic planning would be concerned with those aspects of technology important to the company's business, whether these be construction and fabrication methods in home building, fuel economy in engine manufacturing or packaging methods for consumer products. Systems planning focuses its technological analysis on computers and data communications. Given the complexity of today's equipment and software, the systems planner must be acquainted with a broad technological area, but it is nonetheless parochial when compared to that which preoccupies the corporate planner.

TECHNOLOGICAL CONSIDERATIONS

We have asserted that information systems technology is advancing with great rapidity and that this pace of change is one of the contributing factors to an increased emphasis on systems planning. Technological forecasting as an element in systems planning is perhaps the least difficult factor to contend with. Within a planning period of, let us say, five years, major technological developments in the form of new equipment and software product introductions can be fairly readily identified and anticipated. This is becoming increasingly so as major computer manufacturers introduce new "generations" of computer hardware. Unlike past announcements, in which new computers like the IBM System 360 rendered earlier equipment obsolete, vendors now take pains to assure that new products are compatible with earlier machines in order to protect existing customer bases. Users thus can have confidence that their existing portfolios of computer applications will operate on the new equipment even though they may not exploit all hardware and software features.

Assuming a five year planning period, virtually all new products, whether these be processors, storage devices or terminals, that will come on the market are already in the product planning or engineering stage. Some manufacturers will talk willingly about their research and development efforts while others are more guarded in discussing product features prior to public announcement, but there are independent research firms and consultants who follow the computer industry and produce very reliable forecasts of future configurations and prices. Many of these studies go beyond technology to deal with marketing strategy, government policy and other matters to give their clients valuable insights into new products and services. (2)

One aspect of technology assessment of interest in planning is the degree of volatility exhibited by particular branches of computer technology. As a rule, the older the subtechnology, the less likelihood of major changes in performance characteristics. For example, punched card input-output equipment has changed little over the past twenty years. And studies have shown that the price-performance ratios of large-scale computing equipment have shown a less marked improvement in recent years than those of the newer minicomputers.

All this does not mean, of course, that there are no uncertainties in gauging the future impact of technology, especially when software as well as hardware developments are taken into account. There remains uncertainty about which potential new products will gain acceptance and prove cost effective and which will not. And there will obviously be questions about the suitability of new technology within the systems environment of a particular organization. A law firm in a single city location will have an entirely different perspective on the technology now coming to be associated with the automated office than a national manufacturer with dozens of plant sites and hundreds of marketing offices. Thus, it is not enough simply to become conversant with what new equipment and software may be forthcoming; this must be related to the unique problems and requirements of the organization.

Many organizations that have evolved large centralized data processing facilities in search of economies of scale are now considering more decentralized operating modes employing minicomputers and microprocessors at user locations. The technology to permit such distributed processing, and to make it cost effective, is rapidly becoming available. This does not, however, mean that a distributed processing strategy is the right one in all situations. Centralized processing may still be best for some, or a hierarchical configuration in which central processors coexist with smaller distributed equipment.

Finally, it should be noted that while the future boundaries of technology may be known to those within the computer industry and to the analysts who follow it, such knowledge will not be factored into a company's strategic plan unless a positive effort is made to acquire technological information and determine how technology should be applied. One of the values of formalized planning is that it forces the systems staff to become conversant with new technology and to focus its thinking about how such technology should be utilized.

Despite the acceleration of change, the knowledgeable systems planner can take a fairly accurate fix on what the technology is going to be like over the next few years. It is not easy to take such a reading, not nearly so easy as in the relatively tranquil past, but it can be done. To do so requires much greater awareness of the state of the art with respect to unannounced products than is present in most organizations.

Technology assessment can be a powerful competitive weapon, in that it enables an organization to anticipate technological trends at an early stage and, as a consequence, introduce new technology and develop new applications in advance of competitors not engaged in such assessment.

ENVIRONMENTAL CONSIDERATIONS

Just as future technological capability needs to be identified, there must be a comparable understanding of the forces of change at work in the environment within which systems planning must take place. The environment in which future systems activities are to be conducted has two distinct but related aspects. One has to do with the internal workings of the organization as they affect information systems needs, and the other with the broader environmental situation within which the organization itself must operate.

External environmental factors aside, there are numerous phenomena within the confines of the organization that impact systems planning. A change in the organizational location of the systems function, such as a shift in reporting relationship from the company comptroller to the chief executive officer, would undoubtedly affect at least some strategic goals. And a series of recurring losses, with an adverse effect on budgets for new applications, would alter both goals and timetables for implementation. Other occurrences that could affect systems plans range from relocation of company operations to changes in accounting methods. Many of these internal environmental factors can be identified, and perhaps to some degree controlled, by the systems staff; others, which may have either a salutary or negative effect on systems plans, are difficult to anticipate let alone control.

Changes in the external environment are so multitudinous that they almost defy description. They include shifts in the purchasing and consuming proclivities of the firm's customers, changes which may in themselves be the result of technological change within the customer organization or in his business environment. Strategies of competitors loom as important environmental considerations, especially since many competitive strategies may be based upon exploitation of computer technology. The rate of new product introduction that characterizes many areas of industry, from consumer goods to new financial services and industrial products, underlines the importance of reflecting in the systems plan a profile of the environment in which the organization must function.

For these reasons, an assessment must be made of the business environment to supplement that dealing with computer technology. Environmental considerations can affect systems goals in several respects:

1. Dictate a requirement for major new applications.

2. Cause a major change either upward or downward in resources available for application development.

3. Cause an increase or decline in the size of data bases and transaction processing volume.

4. Require a major rework or integration of existing systems.

5. Necessitate the closing of an existing computer facility or the startup of a new one.

6. Engender changes in personnel management practices, such as the hiring of new specialists, changes in training programs and promoting practices or staff reduction.

Other potential impacts could be cited. But those mentioned indicate the importance of trying to take into account both internal and external environmental factors.

POLICY CONSIDERATIONS

The third major variable affecting the systems plan concerns the policy dictates of top management. What is the firm's competitive strategy going to be over the planning period? Is it to be one of diversification of product line? Are acquisitions, which themselves may have substantial systems capability, contemplated? Will the company be seeking aggressively to enhance its share of market, or is it content to maintain its current position and defend the status quo? Regardless of whether broad corporate goals such as these are expressly stated or must be inferred from management's present actions and past performance, they can have a fundamental effect on any systems plan.

Some planners believe that corporate strategy dictates policy, yet many organizations can be found that lack well articulated corporate strategy but nonetheless have pronounced policy positions. One tenet universally accepted today is that company policy cannot be based simplistically on maximizing return on investment. In particular, there is recognition that corporate goals and policies must be related to the social and economic well-being of the community in which the organization operates.

Certain policies can have a direct and immediate impact on systems planning. A policy of expansion through mergers and acquisitions will have the consequence of requiring systems managers to integrate disparate systems groups and equipment, often with horrendous problems in hardware and software compatability.

Difficulties can also arise if policy mandates that growth be achieved through diversification rather than expansion of existing product lines. The new products may require totally different kinds of support from that which the systems staff has been accustomed to providing.

Even if policy merely demands that the company remain competitive within its existing product and service areas, there are systems planning implications. Should the company endeavor to be innovative in the systems realm in order to improve its products and services and thus enhance its share of market? This is the type of issue that confronted the airline industry some years ago when decisions were made to set up electronic reservation systems, and that commercial banks had to resolve in deciding to automate demand deposit accounting. Many organizations that have adopted an innovative systems strategy have come ruefully to appreciate the saying that "the earliest Christians get the hungriest lions." However, to lag too far behind the competition, especially in industries in which the computer is being integrated into mainstream activities, is to run the risk of falling dangerously behind.

Not all company policies have a major or dramatic impact on computer operations, but need to be taken into account nonetheless in systems planning. For example, a strong policy of equal employment opportunity for minorities must be reflected in plans for recruiting, training and career development of systems professionals.

1.4 CONCEPTUAL ASPECTS OF PLANNING

After a somewhat hectic -- and controversial -- incubation period, systems planning has begun to show signs of maturation as a reasonably well-defined and generally accepted aspect of business management. This is due in part to the expanding body of theory that is helping to provide a conceptual underpinning for successful applications in practice. Some of this work is oriented toward business planning in general; more recent efforts have focused specifically on systems planning.

In order to outline the conceptual basis for systems planning, we will summarize a few of the more significant conceptual views of planning.

A FRAMEWORK FOR PLANNING

There is agreement among most authorities on planning that the basic process is hierarchical in nature, though perspectives vary regarding the numbers and characteristics of levels of planning. Anthony, in his influential work on planning, asserts that there are two distinct types of planning in any organization -- one a high level form of planning concerned with such matters as goal setting and policy formulation and the other associated with the on-going administration of the organization.

Anthony goes on to identify three levels of planning and control as follows:

1. Strategic planning, which has to do with deciding on organizational goals, the resources to attain these goals and the policies associated with goals and resources.

2. Management control, the process by which managers assure that resources are obtained and used effectively and efficiently in the accomplishment of the organization's objectives. This level contains a mixture of planning and control activities.

3. Operational control, the process of assuring that specific tasks are carried out effectively and efficiently. (3)

This conceptual framework is illustrated in Figure 1-4, in which top management, at the apex of the pyramid, is concerned principally with the allocation of resources to achieve corporate goals, middle management is responsible for the effective application of resources and operational management, depicted at the bottom, is engaged in consumption of resources.

Systems planning, depending upon the nature of the planning activity being undertaken, could bisect all three of these levels of planning and control. It is important for planners to recognize just what level of planning and control they are dealing with, and what level of managerial involvement and support they consequently must seek, to assure effective accomplishment of plans.

It should, of course, be noted that Anthony's three levels provide merely a conceptual framework for looking at planning. In some organizations, a different hierarchy might be more appropriately identified, say one reflecting two levels of activity, or four. It should be noted further that in the real world of large decentralized organizations, there are in fact *multiple* planning hierarchies that need to be taken into account, e.g., those at the corporate staff level and those in semi-

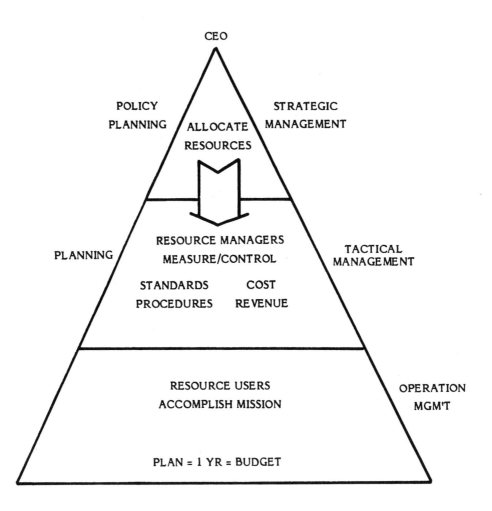

Figure 1-4/Advanced Planning Framework

autonomous divisions or operating subsidiaries. Each is likely to have its own systems needs and unique managerial approaches to planning and control.

LEVELS OF DATA USAGE

Anthony's conceptual framework has been extended and applied specifically to systems planning in a previous work by the author which maps the evolution of business data processing systems in a hierarchical schematic. In most companies there has grown up over a period of many years a variety of data processing applications like those shown in the bottom portion of Figure 1-5. Generally, these have been developed in a piecemeal fashion, with systems analysts and programmers assigned to a new project whenever a current one was completed, and so gradually implementing a series of applications. Typically, the computer was first justified for a single major application, with this key application varying from one industry to another. For example, in a public utility computers were first installed to perform customer billing and in a bank to perform demand deposit accounting, these being the companies' high volume accounting operations and hence offering significant cost justification for computer processing.

Once a company had successfully computerized one or two of these basic applications, it was logical to venture into other application areas. Often, for example, payroll became a candidate for processing, followed by other applications depending upon the priorities set by a given company. Considerable progress was achieved in this way, but it was made haphazardly. Applications were not designed to permit intercommunication among them, even though in the real life environment of company operations there was a significant interaction among the parts of the organization whose activities had become computerized.

Another problem with the step-by-step evolution of applications is that the resultant systems are uneven in quality. Not surprisingly, the first applications computerized, at a time when most companies had little data processing experience, were not very sophisticated or efficient. As data processing applications expanded and evolved, there was in most companies an unevenness in their quality, ranging from excellent to very marginal in design concept and operational performance.

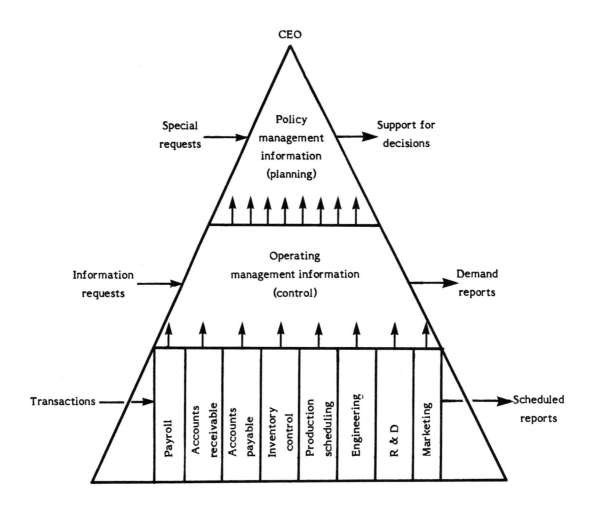

Figure 1-5/Levels of Data Usage

A further characteristic of business data processing systems, as they have e-volved, is that they are *transaction oriented;*that is, they are concerned primarily with capturing and processing the day-to-day operating transactions of the company. In a public utility, computers are dedicated to maintaining the status of customer accounts, with the main input being receipts from customer billing operations. In a commercial bank, there are systems concerned with maintaining the checking accounts of bank customers, capturing and posting individual checks as they clear through the banking system. A manufacturing company utilizes systems to maintain the status of inventory, with stock records for each inventory item controlled by the computer.

These systems are intrinsically low level in nature, having replaced the most routine clerical functions. This is not surprising, for it was in these operations that there was the largest clerical workforce, and hence the most compelling cost justification for computerization. Moreover, such applications were relatively easy to computerize, since the decision rules for these routine functions were usually well defined.

At first, these were not serious limitations for two reasons: 1) Despite the draw-backs, management could appreciate the considerable benefits of using computers for routine data processing tasks; and 2) because the tasks that were first comput-erized were the most routine, the amount of information produced that was of interest to management was minimal. But management's attitude has been chang-ing.

Managers now desire computerized information for the purpose of more effective-ly planning and controlling company operations. The middle and upper portions of Figure 1-5 suggest schematically this shift in emphasis toward serving policy-making mangement at the top level and operating management at the middle level of the organization. These managers are interested in more timely and meaning-ful information for purposes of, respectively, devising future plans and controlling day-to-day operations.

From a planning standpoint, managerial usage of information has several aspects that differentiate it from data usage for operational purposes. For one thing, not all the detail generated by data processing at the lowest level is needed by management. Instead, some subset is required, with this subset varying according to the level of managerial usage. This is suggested schematically in Figure 1-5 by the upward pointing arrows.

It has been said that this is nothing more than a restatement of the time honored principle of "management by exception," and in a sense this is true. However, contemporary information systems are capable of going far beyond the mechanical production of summary reports in a hierarchical fashion in which less and less detail is provided as the level of the recipient goes higher. It is still useful, though, to think in terms of exception reporting, and today's planning approaches are certainly not inconsistent with this principle. Rather, they offer significant extensions to it.

Another feature of managerial usage of information, suggested by the horizontal input and output arrows in Figure 1-5, is that the system must be capable of responding to information requests at the time management requires the information. Managerial input to the system does not, unlike lower-level transactions, constitute a large volume of detail that must be captured and maintained. Instead, there may be relatively few inquiries made by management personnel. But when one is received, the need for information is usually immediate.

Because of the piecemeal approach to application development that has typified past company efforts, the data associated with most existing applications are not especially suitable for usage within a management information system. Hence, a planned restructuring of data bases is usually required. (4)

OTHER VIEWS

Simon distinguishes between "programmed" and "nonprogrammed" decision making, wherein lower level decisions tend to be programmed in the sense that they are governed by specific rules and procedures while nonprogrammed decisions involve broader and higher level problem solving in which the decision making process is not well structured. (5) In this sense, strategic information systems planning obviously concerns nonprogrammed decisions. If successfully carried out, it should aid in extending the boundaries of programmed decision making throughout the organization.

In his interesting work on systems planning, Blumenthal discusses the relationship between plans and projects by differentiating between the "plan of projects" and the "project plan." The plan of projects is viewed as global, involving a scheduled series of efforts leading to the realization of the totality of systems envisioned within an overall framework. Individual project plans are local in nature and cover specifically defined phases for individual projects. (6)

It is also recognized that planning is not only hierarchical but also iterative, as pointed out by Emery and others. (7) Because there are levels in planning, the strategic plan intended to govern lower level planning will need to be modified as subordinate level planning proceeds, with a resultant questioning of higher level assumptions or with demand for additional implementation resources.

Another reason for iteration in planning has to do with the extended time frame for strategic planning. As implementation of the plan proceeds over time, objectives and resource requirements become more specifically stated and assumptions are disproved or modified. At some point, the original planning premises must be reviewed and updated.

Thus, there is a two dimensional aspect to the iteration of plans, the first resulting from the hierarchical characteristic of planning and the second resulting from modifications dictated by the passage of time as planning goals gain greater specificity.

1.5 UNCERTAINTY IN PLANNING

Another important characteristic of strategic planning is that it must be conducted under conditions of uncertainty. We have identified the basic elements of planning as technological, environmental and policy. Though some aspects of these elements can be accepted as certainties, or at least high probability phenomena, five years or more into the future, many obviously cannot be. This means that future events affecting the systems plan, whether of a technological, environmental or policy nature, cannot be predicted with complete accuracy. The degree of accuracy tends, of course, to lessen as the planning period lengthens. This aspect of the planning process can be likened to an exponential horn as shown in Figure 1-6, in which the area inside the horn represents an estimate as to what future systems are going to be like within the organization.

The possibilities of variation in systems characteristics are fairly narrow in the immediate future, because commitments of equipment and personnel have already been made for operational systems and application development projects. Further along in the planning period the possibilities begin to widen. An organization that does not perform long-range systems planning cannot narrow the possibilities sufficiently to fit within the horn-like area, and consequently is confronted with an overwhelming array of future systems possibilities.

A slightly different way of looking at the planning process is to identify those aspects of future systems that may be viewed as certainties by the straight line symbols in Figure 1-7, and to indicate by the wavy lines conditions of less and less certainty further out along a time scale. Eventually, the future systems capability of the organization must split, amoeba-like, into several different major alternatives since changes, whose effect cannot be accurately gauged, may direct the organization along one of two or three or more significantly different future paths. This diagram could be meaningfully superimposed on the exponential horn, as shown in Figure 1-8, to suggest the possible system configurations that may exist during the planning period.

Recognition of this element of uncertainty in strategic planning suggests the need for contingency planning through the formulation of alternative plans. One of the most serious criticisms of large information systems development projects, especially those described as management information system (MIS) efforts, is that they are often unrealistically broad in scope and consequently may take years to fully implement. This kind of strategy creates a dangerous situation in that management will not know how effectively information systems goals are being carried out until some point in the distant future when the large scale, integrated MIS is scheduled to go on line. Clearly, in such circumstances, it would be prudent

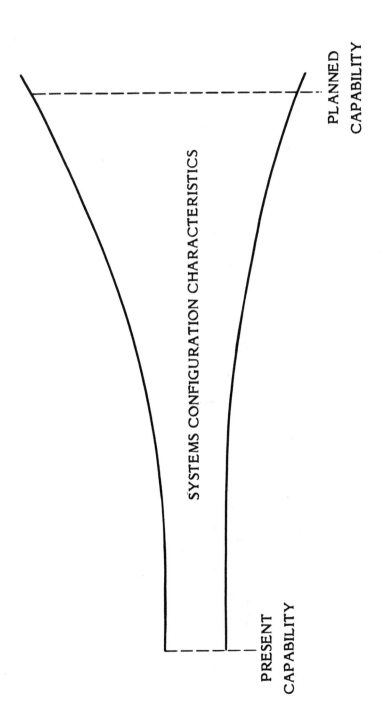

Figure 1-6/Systems Planning Projection

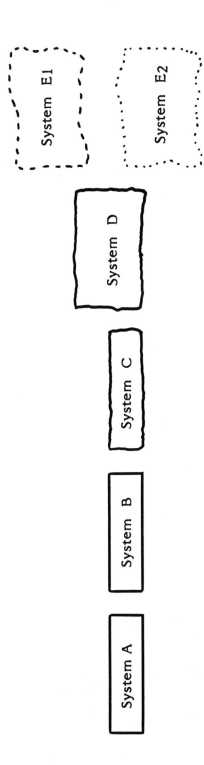

Figure 1-7/Systems Planning Possibilities

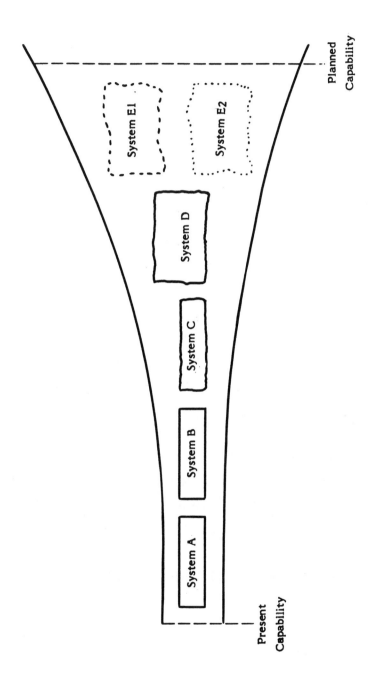

Figure 1-8/Systems Planning Profile

to have alternative plans in case the MIS project is delayed or fails to meet expectations. This is especially true in planning within government agencies where funding for system development requires an annual commitment in the form of appropriations with an opportunity for periodic challenges from critics of policies supported by computer systems. There are numerous case histories in federal government agencies of systems projects that absorbed years of planning effort being abandoned because appropriation requests for procurement of needed equipment were denied.

Some form of risk analysis should be applied to long-range systems plans to gain insight into the consequences of failure to implement plans or serious delay in implementation. What would be the consequences of a decision to abort a major new application development effort at various stages in its life cycle? What is the probability of such an occurrence, considering such factors as the degree of technological uncertainty and other risk factors?

Risk analysis of planning objectives, and projects intended to support these objectives, helps to establish the need for alternative strategies. If project A is considered a high risk venture, there is compelling reason to develop plans for project B as an alternative that could be implemented if necessary.

There must, of course, be a reasonable limit to the number of alternatives that are analyzed and maintained. At minimum, though, plans should be made to perpetuate existing applications and equipment in case resources do not become available to support major new replacement initiatives.

1.6 IS STRATEGIC PLANNING REALLY NECESSARY?

Despite the current emphasis on strategic planning in leading organizations, the question still arises: "Is such planning necessary in all situations?" Are there organizations that, either because of size or the nature of the business, cannot justify the expense of creating and maintaining a strategic plan? The question is pertinent, since an investment in planning may be considerable, ranging from a part-time assignment for one professional staff member up to a unit of several people dedicated to planning.

It is undeniable that very large organizations, with annual data processing expenditures approaching $100 million, not only *can* afford to invest in planning, but would be managerially deficient if they failed to do so. It also seems generally accepted that organizations with data processing budgets greater than $10 million per year should engage in some form of strategic planning. Below that level, a careful analysis may be in order to determine what resources should be allocated to planning.

Size of budget is but one criterion. Are there companies, whether large or small, that have product lines and business operations so invariable from year to year that strategic planning is not necessary? Of a dozen or so organizations, both commercial and public service, represented at a workshop of the Society for Management Information Systems, not one characterized its operations as stable enough to obviate the need for a systems plan.

If the policy dictates of a company are fairly fixed and its business activities relatively stable, there is need for planning to deal with the other elements of change: the technological and environmental. Experience over the past twenty years amply demonstrates that the introduction of new technology can impact the systems activities of even the most staid and conservative organizations. The installation of automated teller terminals in financial institutions, for instance, has transformed their accounting systems from the early computerized batch processing operations that took place in the "back room" to on-line transaction processing employing direct access storage devices and data base management software.

Given the volatile technological and economic environment in which all organizations must operate, it is doubtful that there are many in which strategic planning is not warranted. For example, planners within even a relatively stable government agency such as the U.S. Department of Agriculture have witnessed a dramatic increase in food stamp payments within a five-year period, from under $1 billion to over $8 billion. And systems planners in commercial banks have seen a heightened emphasis in recent years on consumer credit activities in the form of personal lines of credit tied into checking accounts, credit cards and other services demanding increased data processing support, with electronic fund transfer systems looming on the horizon. (8)

There have been unsuccessful attempts to do strategic planning in which expertise was lacking to generate a plan acceptable to top management. In organizations that do not have adequate resources to develop a meaningful plan, substitutes can be sought for a full-fledged formalized planning procedure. The creation of a systems steering committee, consisting of top level executives responsible for major functional areas of the company, can compensate at least in part for formalized planning. Such a committee could meet periodically to review project proposals and budget requests for information systems.

Steering committees were widely prevalent in the early days of business data processing to supervise the conduct of initial "feasibility" studies, but tended to become inactive as experience was gained in computer usage. In the context of strategic planning, though, critical review by senior executives of new initiatives, along with an effort to assign priorities to project proposals, could be highly beneficial. The systems steering committee could seek to assure that new projects are consistent with overall corporate goals even when corporate plans have not been explicityly stated.

1.7 BENEFITS OF PLANNING

The principal benefit inherent in planning is that it *permits the organization to exercise a favorable influence* on future events. But there are collateral benefits to systems planning that should be noted. Some of these can be achieved by other means, but they are valuable by-products of the process of developing and promulgating a systems plan.

1. Enhancing Communications. The systems plan provides a vehicle for communication both upward from the information systems function to top management and downward from the director of information systems to subordinate managers and professionals within the information systems function. In a decentralized organization, the plan can also aid in lateral communication among divisional systems groups. Even where such groups are highly autonomous, they can benefit from an understanding of the strategic goals of their

peers in other parts of the company.

Communication should be two-way in all cases, with opportunities to modify the plan either through top down or bottom up interaction as planning goals are reviewed and become better understood throughout the organization.

2. Obtaining Organizational Commitment. The issuance of an approved information systems plan implies a commitment on the part of top management to support the plan by providing adequate resources and on the part of the systems staff to apply their best efforts to achieving mutually agreed upon goals. The plan can thus be viewed as a sort of compact between top management and the systems function which provides a basis for reviewing the performance of the systems staff in attaining agreed upon goals.

3. Establishing Constraints. An information systems plan that reflects the goals and policies of top management will provide a constraining mechanism on the allocation of resources among systems projects. These planning ground-rules can improve resource allocation by narrowing the set of objectives that might otherwise be selected by systems people and channeling efforts toward those that are potentially most valuable to the organization.

4. Improving Project Selection. With the goals set forth in an information systems plan at the apex of company systems activities, subordinate objectives can be delineated and projects authorized that will most effectively carry out the systems strategy. In the absence of a plan, other criteria will by default be applied to project selection, such as: the size, leverage and budgetary resources of the user groups requesting new services; the "squeaking wheel" approach of remedying the most currently acute systems problems (or at least those that are perceived as being most acute); or the personal proclivities of project personnel who tend to be interested in newer and more exotic applications of technology that do not necessarily offer the greatest benefit to company operations.

5. Controlling Resources. The systems plan permits goals and objectives to be tied in to budget allocations to provide better assurance that dollars are

channeled to those activities that are most relevant to the achievement of strategic goals. This can be especially important in companies in which there is no charge-back of systems costs to end users.

6. Improving Levels of Confidence. Because the information systems plan provides positive direction by means of goals and negative guidance in the form of constraints, there can be greater confidence that goals will be achieved without undue diversion of effort or resources. If a project is known to have a high priority in furthering the systems plan, it is likely to receive the attention and support that it deserves. Given the large scope of many computer projects, and the long lead times for their implementation, it is especially important to have a high level of confidence that there will be timely completion of projects and achievement of design objectives.

7. Managing Technological Change. Change in information systems is inevitable as technology advances and as user demands for information services increase. Without a plan, the systems staff will find itself grappling with a chronic problem of *reacting* to user demands rather than anticipating them and will be unable to provide for the orderly introduction of new technology to satisfy user requests for new services.

NOTES

1. There is no uniformity among planning experts on usage of the words "goal" and "objective." Some, like Ackoff, view goals as being more specific and subordinate to objectives; others use the words interchangeably. Russell L. Ackoff, "A Concept of Corporate Planning," New York, John Wiley and Sons, Inc., 1970, pp. 23-24.

2. Charles P. Lecht provides a good example of such studies in "The Waves of Change" which he subtitles "A Techno-Economic Analysis of the Data Processing Industry," published by Advanced Computer Techniques, 437 Madison Avenue, New York, NY   10022, 1977, 186 pages.

3. Robert N. Anthony, "Planning and Control Systems: A Framework for Analysis," Boston, Graduate School of Business Administration, Harvard University, 1965, pp. 15-18.

4. Robert V. Head, "Manager's Guide to Management Information Systems," Englewood Cliffs, N.J., Prentice-Hall, Inc., 1972, pp. 10-16.

5. Herbert A. Simon, "The New Science of Management Decision," Englewood Cliffs, N.J., Prentice-Hall, Inc., 1977, pp. 45-49.

6. Sherman C. Blumenthal, "Management Information Systems: A Framework for Planning and Development," Englewood Cliffs, N.J., Prentice-Hall, Inc., 1969, pp. 85-100.

7. James C. Emery, "Organizational Planning and Control Systems: Theory and Technology," Toronto, Ontario, the Macmillan Company, 1969, pp. 118-129.

8. A survey by the U.S. General Accounting Office of 18 organizations (14 private corporations, three state governments and a county government) revealed

that "at 15 of the organizations visited, long-range planning is considered important to achieving ADP goals and objectives, as well as business goals and objectives." Long-range plans varied from three to 20 years. "Study by the Staff of the U.S. General Accounting Office," Washington, D.C., AFMD-81-104, October 2, 1981.

Chapter 2
The Organizational Environment

"Every noble work is at first impossible."

-- Thomas Carlyle

Information systems activities have been analyzed by Gibson and Nolan according to four stages of growth.

1. Initiation. This is the stage in which the computer is first introduced into the organization, usually justified on the basis of cost reducing accounting applications.

2. Proliferation. During this stage, early successes lead to a proliferation of additional applications and rapidly increasing data processing costs.

3. Consolidation. At this stage, control measures are applied by a concerned management in an effort to bring computer projects under better control.

4. Integration. Here controls are in place, relations with users improved and more productive and sophisticated applications begin to be developed.

These are illustrated in Figure 2-1 in the form of an "S" curve representing systems expenditures over time.

During the first two stages of growth, planning is virtually nonexistent and budgetary controls are loose. At stage three, strong budgetary control is exerted but it is not until stage four that planning receives more emphasis. (1)

Nolan has more recently extended the original growth stage theory to encompass two additional stages: Data Administration, which concentrates on the sharing of

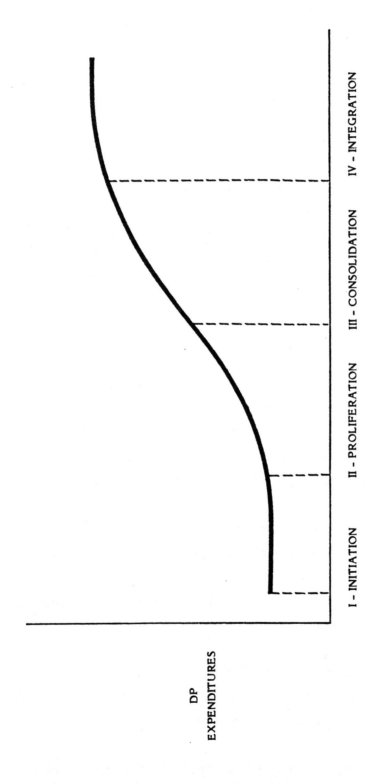

Figure 2-1/Stages of DP Growth

data resources, and Maturity, which matches completed systems with organizational information flows.

To determine the stage that an organization is currently in, Nolan suggests two sets of criteria. The first, which looks at the overall organization, uses two measures: the historical ratio of DP expenditures to organizational growth and the mix of computer technologies in use. The second set separately characterizes each of the four growth areas.

Finally, Nolan has a strategy for how strongly financial and performance management controls should be applied at each strategic growth stage. The balance between control and "slack" (lack of control) determines the rate of computing growth. The proper balance at each stage enables the growth to occur in an orderly fashion. In short, Nolan's theory offers a means for planning how much management control to apply and when to apply it.

Not all company data processing histories exhibit the characteristics outlined by Gibson and Nolan, but there has been a fairly consistent pattern of justifying the computer initially for one major application, such as billing in a public utility, revenue accounting in an airline or demand deposit accounting in a bank, and then proceeding to extend computer operations to other application areas as initial successes are achieved and professional staff expertise is built up. At some point, greater discipline is applied to the systems function, often in the form of project control techniques. This imposition of controls may be due to runaway costs or may result from a system fiasco, such as a major application on which management has been counting that does not perform up to specifications or is seriously delayed in becoming operational.

Usually, the twin factors of rising data processing costs and extension of computer processing into vital company functions, such as the booking of airline reservations, underscore the need for better planning and control. This, in turn, provides a base of planning experience and a stimulus to creation of longer range plans.

Of course, the introduction of strategic planning early in a company's history of computer usage would help to avoid the cost overruns and mismanaged projects that most organizations have had to endure. Unfortunately, planning is not generally understood and accepted until an evolutionary process like that described in Gibson and Nolan has run its course.

2.1 SCOPE OF SYSTEMS PLANNING

The introduction of information systems technology within both public and commercial organizations over the past twenty years has been characterized by a dramatic expansion of the role of the computer from its initial acquisition to perform fairly limited processing tasks. Expansion of the scope of computer operations involves more, however, than a proliferation of applications; it implies as well an extension of computer capabilities upward within the company hierarchy to aid in managerial decision making.

Accompanying this increase in both the range and level of computer usage has been a concommitant expansion in the responsibility of the information systems director. At the onset of computer activity, the data processing manager typically reported to the company controller. Today it is common for information systems operations to be directed by a corporate vice president for information systems reporting to the chief executive officer. In government there are similar positions in many agencies at the level of a deputy assistant secretary charged specifically with data processing responsibility.

In view of the expanding role of the computer, it is realistic to define the boundaries of information systems planning fairly broadly. Planning efforts should unquestionably extend beyond data processing to include data communications, in reflection of the growing emphasis on distributed processing and terminal usage. In many organizations, information systems planning covers not only the data processing applications associated with automating clerical and white collar functions but includes factory automation through computerized industrial process control and laboratory instrumentation in which minicomputers are imbedded.

In office automation, the computer is playing an increasingly dominant part in the evolving concept of the paperless office. Word processing equipment for the storage and production of textual information with the aid of minicomputers provides an example of devices previously considered office products like the typewriter and dictating machine but which are now viewed as elements in an overall information processing network, linked perhaps to large computers located elsewhere in the organization.

Thus, as information systems technology continues to advance beyond its initial limited applications, the scope of systems planning must be broadened accordingly. It is difficult to demarcate just what the ultimate boundaries of computer usage within the organization may be, but it is incumbent on those engaged in strategic planning to define their goals broadly.

2.2 INFORMATION RESOURCES MANAGEMENT

The newly emerging concept of Information Resources Management (IRM) reinforces the desirability of a broadly scoped strategic plan. The basic tenet of IRM is that information is not a free good. It is instead a costly and valuable organizational asset that requires application of the same basic managerial principles and approaches that are now applied in business organizations to their other major resources -- people, dollars and facilities. As organizations become more complex and move toward on-line data bases, information becomes not just an important resource; it becomes perhaps the most crucial resource.

IRM is of importance to systems planners because it represents a potential integrating force for a variety of activities heretofore managed separately. From an advanced planning standpoint, IRM has three salient characteristics.

First, IRM is a *function*. It is a clustering together of tasks that any organization must perform in an orderly manner to plan and control activities relating to the handling of information, regardless of whether this information is digitally stored or otherwise recorded and maintained. In this respect, IRM is a function closely akin to other resource management functions such as personnel, finance and inventory control.

Second, IRM is an *analytical concept*. By capturing, identifying, measuring, and evaluating both information handling costs and information handling values in a single, integrated framework, companies can better see how the benefits relate to the costs and where possible tradeoffs can be considered between comparatively less efficient and effective approaches and more efficient and effective ones.

Third, IRM is a *body of knowledge*. It is admittedly still developing but its emergence is beyond dispute. IRM is multidisciplinary, cutting across such fields as economics, business administration, information processing and library science.

IRM allows management to see what information is really costing, and what its true value is, in the same accounting, budgeting, and control formats that managers are accustomed to seeing. Under IRM, information is no longer treated primarily as an overhead or indirect cost, but rather as a direct organizational resource that is broken out like other organizational resources, e.g., people, dollars, inventories. By using such an analytical approach, operating managers must explain, defend and justify their information resource requirements the same way they defend their dollar requirements, their personnel requirements and their plant and facility needs.

IRM also provides a means of integrating increasingly complex, costly and sohpisticated computer, telecommunications, micrographic, reprographic and other information handling technologies -- to harness them as a single team, for the achievement of planning goals. IRM provides the harmonizing environment that permits these important information tools to emerge from a suboptimal status to one approaching full optimization. Thus, IRM does not replace MIS or DBMS or other approaches; instead, it permits these established information management techniques to come to full fruition.

Better safeguards are available through IRM for the protection of personally-identifiable or company sensitive data -- protection from both fraudulent or inadvertent disclosure to unauthorized persons. This is because IRM stresses the need to assign specific parameters to all of the company's information flows and holdings, such as: who are the authorized users who should be given access; what is the degree of sensitivity of a particular company recordkeeping or reporting system; and who is accountable for data protection, data quality and data integrity. At present, too many company information handling practices are haphazard when it comes to systematically identifying and putting in place these information security parameters. Often there is no "need to know" parameter whatsoever. Or responsibility for data quality and integrity is not specified in a way that data suppliers and handlers can be held accountable for meeting information quality standards.

To the planner, IRM affords a real opportunity for making tradeoffs between information-intensive approaches to achieving organizational goals — approaches that may well be cheaper than energy-intensive or capital-intensive or labor-intensive approaches. By placing the organization's information resources organically into its planning, budgeting and control formats, alongside other organizational resources, the CEO and his top management team, as well as middle management, can see where and how important tradeoffs might be effected. (2)

2.3 SYSTEMS PLANNING AND CORPORATE PLANNING

Within the past twenty-five years many leading companies have formalized the process of corporate strategic planning. There has been an accompanying increase in the literature on corporate planning and a proliferation in techniques and methods to aid in corporate planning. Financial modeling is, for example, now widespread as is technological forecasting which itself employs a whole array of specialized techniques.

Beyond the growing recognition by management that better planning is needed to eliminate uncontrolled systems growth, the availability of corporate plans and planning methodologies has stimulated the creation of information systems plans. In many instances, planning is mandated from the top for the information systems function along with all other major organizational components.

In a well articulated planning environment, there is a flow of guidance downward from top management by means of statements of goals and policies that provide a framework for information systems planning and other kinds of subordinate plans. There is then a flow of planning information back upward in the form of the draft strategic information systems plan submitted for management review and approval. This completes a planning feedback loop in which planning initiatives at the top trigger lower level action which in turn is conveyed back to top management. Figure 2-2 depicts a planning structure in which user requirements are reflected in a systems plan which is then integrated in summary form into the company business plan.

Unfortunately, there are many organizations in which such an ideal situation does not prevail. In these circumstances, it is still possible to do effective planning from the bottom up. Here, the systems staff would initiate a draft strategic plan and seek approval from higher management.

Some system specialists become distraught at working in such a planning environment, feeling that planning cannot be done in a vacuum. One planner asserts, for example, that:

> A long-range plan for data processing, without a long-range company plan, is nonsense. I have been appalled at the attempts I have witnessed to develop plans for a data processing installation in the absence of any sound plan for the corporation, or business entity, as a whole .... The responsibility of data processing is to support the company business plan. The authority for data processing to fulfill that responsibility is vested in the company business plan and can never be considered separately. (3)

Actually, the absence of top-down guidance need not create such a grim picture. In bottom-up planning, a feedback loop can exist in which planning is initiated by the information systems staff with the results pyramided upward for higher lever review and approval. Assuming that management carefully reviews strategic systems goals, there can then be a reaction conveyed downward to the systems planners who can revise their plans accordingly.

This is not to suggest that a bottom-up approach is as good as top-down planning. It is not. Plans produced in this manner may not give adequate recognition to

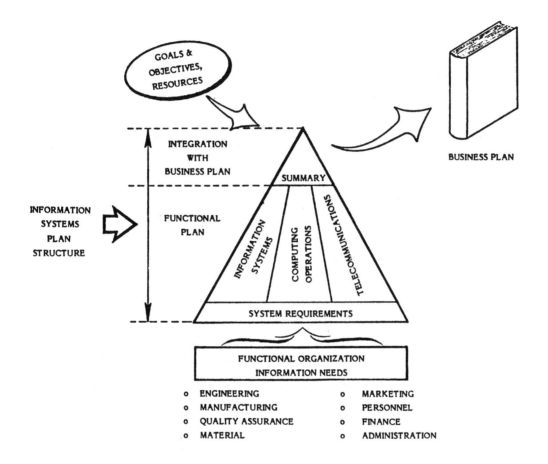

Figure 2-2/Business Planning and Systems Planning

unstated company goals and policies, especially if the top management review is perfunctory. And it is doubtless more difficult for systems people to try to take into account corporate goals and policies that are not explicitly stated.

When the company director of information systems attains top management rank, as is the case in many companies, the question of top-down versus bottom-up planning becomes somewhat academic. A vice president for information systems reporting to the company president is in fact a member of top management and should be able to convey corporate planning goals to his staff as an input to the systems planning process. Similarly, the presence of a systems steering committee consisting of top level line managers can provide meaningful linkage between corporate plans and systems plans.

Another means of compensating for lack of corporate planning strategy is to develop a set of *planning assumptions*. These would concern the environment in which the organization is expected to be operating as well as policies that are to be followed. Such assumptions about a company's future direction might cover a diversity of factors such as growth in sales volume, product mix, plant location, size of work force, government regulation and activities of the competition.

If a systems plan is devised in the absence of corporate planning activity, the goals and assumptions contained in the plan should be presented to top management in an effort to gain endorsement or aid in modifying those portions of the plan that are unrealistic. This means that the systems plan, or at least that portion of it dealing with goals and assumptions, should be in a format and language intelligible to general managers not conversant with computer technology.

A troublesome problem in systems planning confronts federal, state and some local government agencies during the transition from one elected administration to another. In this environment, there is not only a change in the chief executive in the form of a new president, governor or mayor, but also a turnover in the heads and assistant heads of "cabinet level" agencies. This problem is compounded by the fact that the goals of the incoming administration are frequently antithetical to those of the managers who are being replaced. Thus, the policies that have governed information systems may be subject to drastic overhaul and even reversal. This situation is roughly analogous to a corporate systems manager discovering one day that his entire managerial hierarchy from board chairman through assistant vice president had suddenly resigned and been replaced by a totally different managerial group.

2.4 SYSTEMS PLANNING AND BUDGETING

It is desirable to tie systems planning into budgeting either loosely or directly. This is done in some cases to the extent that the budget year constitutes the first year of the system plan. The systems plan itself then contains two levels of detail, a longer range section containing strategic goal statements, constraints and assumptions accompanied by much more specific information about immediate plans and objectives for the budget year.

In other instances, the systems plan contains detailed information about objectives and dollar resources for information systems for the current budget year plus the coming year, with long-range planning information covering the period beyond the second year.

There are difficulties in closely coupling strategic planning and budgeting. For one thing, the expense categories used in formulating the budget may not be the most appropriate ones for system planning purposes. For instance, a budget category covering outside contracts may need to be broken down according to consulting, time sharing service, software packages and contract programming to be meaningful in planning. Or, equipment rentals may need to be differentiated to distinguish between remote devices and equipment at a central processing site.

These specialized requirements have led in some cases to a duality in budget formulation and reporting whereby two breakdowns of expenditures are produced, one conforming to overall company budget procedures and the other broken down into categories more useful in systems planning. This is the case within the federal government where information systems costs are included in gross terms as a component of appropriation requests for each mission of the agency but are compiled separately to detail expenditures for personnel, equipment rentals, supplies, etc. for purposes of systems management. If budget preparation and accounting are computerized, there may be little problem in assuring that the specialized systems budget categories "cross foot" to the overall budget and that expenses are distributed according to two classifications.

As the organization enters into each new annual budget preparation cycle, it faces the task of reconciling the systems plan against the realities of budgetary resource allocations and the imposition of spending constraints. This involves two kinds of activity. First, the goals in the systems plan beyond the current budget year serve as input to preparation of next year's budget request. Then, to the extent that budgets are reduced or funds reallocated among projects, the longer range plan will have to be revised. This can be an especially important exercise if changes are dictated in capital investment budgets with a consequent effect on long-range plans geared to replacing or augmenting computing equipment.

In seeking to link planning and budgeting, it may be useful to stagger the planning cycles so that the system plan is reviewed and updated *before* the start of budget formulation and can thus serve as guidance to those developing the information systems budget. For example, one organization prepares its information systems plan in the fall, including detailed estimates of expenses for two years, and begins its budget preparation activity in early spring of the following year.

Where the expenses of information systems operations are charged back to end users, there must be a mechanism for providing these users with advance information about potential increases in their billings, such as might occur if there were a major new equipment procurement. If detailed, short-range information system planning precedes budget preparation, realistic cost estimates can be generated as input to budget preparation by the various user departments.

Some form of "zero base budgeting" (ZBB) may be appropriate in reviewing both on-going computer operations as well as planned applications. Here, all systems activities -- both operational as well as planned -- are reviewed annually to determine whether their continuation or initiation is justified. Short of adopting the somewhat complex methodology of ZBB, a simpler kind of project prioritization may be useful in budgeting as well as planning. We will consider this further in the next section.

As a general premise, it is desirable — despite complexities and scheduling problems -- to relate systems planning to budgeting in some fashion. If the information systems plan exists entirely independent of annual operating plans, there is a danger that strategic goals may be overlooked or ignored as resources are allocated among competing requirements and that the systems objectives formulated in annual operating plans may be inconsistent with broader goals.

2.5 SYSTEMS PLANNING AND PROJECT PLANNING

Project selection and project management have an integral relationship to strategic planning. Individual computer projects, whether large or small, provide the means for realizing the goals of strategic planning. As we have noted, a goal may engender one or more objectives which in turn lead to the establishment of systems development projects.

PROJECT SELECTION

There is a considerable literature devoted to computer project selection. (4) In determining which projects to authorize, management is usually confronted with a classic resource allocation problem since there are fewer resources, i.e., men, money and machines, than there are proposals for new applications. The problem is especially acute in organizations that do not charge back for systems services. It is also troublesome in organizations with a good deal of maturity in computer usage which must devote substantial effort to maintaining existing applications. This means that fewer resources are available to apply to new projects.

Figure 2-3 illustrates this managerial dilemma in mature systems organizations in which maintenance of a growing portfolio of operational applications consumes a large proportion of available dollar resources (more than 50% in many cases). Thus, even though the systems budget may be increasing over time, there are still not enough resources available to fully satisfy user demand.

Many techniques have been devised to assign priorities among competing projects. The use of a systems steering committee is one method. Here, users could be required to rank new project proposals on the assumption that funding will not

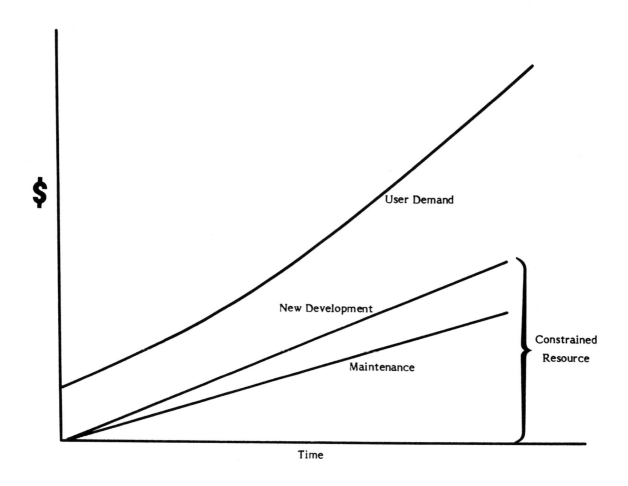

Figure 2-3/The Resource Allocation Problem

be available for all projects. Final priorities would then be established by the steering committee based on a review of all project proposals.

This can be a difficult decision process when there is no chargeback procedure for systems costs, and users regard information systems as a "free good" in formulating their requests for additional services. The application of cost/benefit analysis to rank projects can aid in project selection. In some instances, this has been refined to reflect project "profitability" in which elaborate quantitative methods are applied to determine return on investment. (5)

The systems plan can serve as the point of departure for assigning priorities. Projects can be reviewed according to the extent to which they contribute to planning objectives and are consistent with planning constraints and assumptions. With the strategic plan as the guide, other techniques such as systems steering committee review and cost-benefit analysis can then be applied within an overall planning framework

Figure 2-4 provides a listing of priority criteria that have been applied by various organizations to select new systems projects. These are not listed in order of importance, but are shown merely to illustrate the scope and variety of selection criteria. In actual practice, an organization should choose a subset of such criteria -- perhaps five or six -- that are most relevant to its particular systems environment. These could then be weighted or otherwise quantified to derive numerical "scores" for selection purposes. But regardless of the extent to which prioritization ranking is quantified, managerial judgement must ultimately be applied in making resource allocation decisions.

In many large organizations, project selection in furtherance of planning goals is complicated by a pattern of decentralization in which systems resources are not lodged in a single unit. If each decentralized operating division has its own systems staff, the question arises whether projects will be selected and developed independently by these units or whether there will be guidance and control from headquarters.

This problem really extends beyond project selection; it concerns where the basic

1. Direct Cost-Savings or Displacement
2. Inadequate Current DP System (Requiring "Fix")
3. Primary High-Volume Application (Transaction Driven)
4. Availability of Funds
5. Improved User Services
6. Enhanced Fiscal Control
7. Proven Application in Industry
8. Established Current DP Practice
9. Low Marginal Additional Cost
10. Availability of Computerized Data Files
11. Legal/Policy Imposition (Mandatory)
12. Problems in Processing Manually
13. Supports Organizational Objectives
14. Displacement of Archaic DP Equipment
15. Low Risk of Failure
16. Assurance of Timely Completion
17. Predecessor to Other Systems

Figure 2-4/Priority Criteria For New Systems Initiatives

responsibility for adherence to planning goals will lie. If each division is allowed to proceed autonomously to develop its own applications, in furtherance of its own goals, a condition of *suboptimal* usage of systems resources will inevitably arise. From the standpoint of corporate strategy, the highest priority project for Division A may be lower in value than the third ranked project from Division B. This means that valuable resources will not be allocated optimally, though, of course, there may be other compelling reasons for allowing the divisional autonomy that causes the suboptimization.

It is possible to permit divisional flexibility in project selection by establishing dollar thresholds beyond which headquarters approval would be required for the initiation of a project. One organization with a total systems budget of over $100 million sets this threshold at $25,000; another, with a smaller budget, sets $5,000 as the limit.

We have been considering the matter of project planning for work to be done by systems professionals. Yet increasingly, with the advent of terminals and data networks, new applications are being developed by users on their own with little assistance from the professional staff. This is especially likely to take place in an environment in which users are permitted to acquire minicomputers for their own applications. Applications developed by users in this way may not have the magnitude to be of great concern to management in controlling new systems projects. However, as terminals and minicomputers proliferate, with simplified and easily learned "user friendly" programming languages, more and more resources may in this way be diverted from the purview of formalized planning and control.

The issues we have been discussing, i.e., decentralization of the systems function and central staff review of divisional project plans, represent policy matters that must be resolved by top management. Their resolution will provide guidelines that can then be reflected in company-wide strategic systems planning.

LARGE PROJECT MANAGEMENT

At the opposite extreme from an environment in which there are numerous projects, many perhaps quite small in scope and conducted in an "open shop" atmosphere, is the situation in which a single project dominates all other systems activity and requires the bulk of the organization's resources for implementation. Many development efforts labelled as "management information systems" have this characteristic, in which an effort is mounted to integrate various major subsystems into a single system to support managerial decision making at various levels within the organization and within various functional components such as marketing, manufacturing and warehousing.

Some massive projects involving transaction processing have this same characteristic of dominating the planning and resource allocation process. Airline reservation systems of a generation ago provide a good example. For years, the airline industry struggled -- almost to the exclusion of other computer projects -- to develop large terminal networks with computerized flight information, seat inventory control and electronically stored passenger records. Similarly, commercial banks went through a major -- and traumatic -- epoch in automating demand deposit accounting and are now on the threshold of an even more ambitious effort to implement electronic fund transfer systems. In government, there are many examples of dominant and all encompassing systems in such agencies as the Internal Revenue Service, Social Security Administration and the logistics activities of the Department of Defense. In a one-project organization, the strategic plan and the project plan become one and the same with the single overriding goal being successful completion of the project.

An important characteristic of large projects, that allies project planning closely with strategic planning, is that a project may extend beyond the duration of the budget year and thus require an advance commitment of resources. This means that the risks in undertaking such long-term projects must be taken into account by strategic planners, as there is the possibility -- indeed, some would say, the finite probability -- of overruns in costs and schedules.

LIFE CYCLE MANAGEMENT

Today, the concept of life cycle management is being applied increasingly to large systems projects. This involves the identification of standard phases for all projects and the application of planning and control measures appropriate to each phase. Before a project is allowed to proceed from one phase to another, with an attendant commitment of resources, certain criteria must be met. For example, "deliverables" in the form of acceptable documentation must be produced before the project is authorized to continue. Figure 2-5 provides an illustration of a project life cycle based on federal information processing standards issued by the National Bureau of Standards. (6) Here three major phases in a project are defined:

1. Initiation. During the initiation phase, the objectives and a general definition of the requirements are established. Feasibility studies, cost/benefit analyses and user requirements documentation are prepared within this phase.

2. Development. During the development phase, detailed requirements are determined and software is defined, specified, programmed and tested. Documentation is prepared within this phase to provide an adequate record of the technical information developed.

3. Operation. During the operation phase, the software is maintained, evaluated and changed as additional requirements are identified.

The critical development phase consists of stages that produce a pre-defined set of documentation:

1. Definition. During the definition stage, the requirements for software are determined. Functional requirements and data requirements documents are prepared.

2. Design. During the design stage, design alternatives and specific functions to be performed are analyzed and a design is specified. Documents include system/subsystem specifications, program specifications, data base specifications and a test plan.

3. Programming. During the programming stage, the software is coded and debugged. Documents prepared during this stage include the users manual, program maintenance manual and test plan.

Initiation Phase	Development Phase				Operation Phase
	Definition Stage	Design Stage	Programming Stage	Testing Stage	
Feasibility Study Document	Functional Requirements Document	System/Subsystem Specification	Users Manual	Test Analysis Report	Maintenance Document
Cost Benefit Analysis	Data Requirements Document	Program Specification	Operations Manual	Project Acceptance Report	
		Data Base Specification	Program Maintenance Manual		
		Test ——— Plan			
Management Approval	Management and Technical Approval	Management and Technical Approval	Technical Approval	Technical Approval	Management and Technical Approval

Figure 2-5/Project Life Cycle

4. Test. During the test stage, the software is tested and related documentation reviewed. The software and documentation are evaluated in terms of readiness for implementation.

Under life cycle management, each phase and stage calls for various levels of managerial review at specific junctures in the project. Figure 2-6 shows key activities during the initiation phase and relates these to the preparation of three document types associated with this phase. Each of the subsequent phases has a similar well-defined set of activities and document types.

Though it would be impractical to apply formalized life cycle management controls to minor projects, the approach can be useful in documenting large-scale project plans and relating them to the strategic plan.

2.6 LEVELS OF PLANNING

As we stated in Chapter 1, corporate planning is hierarchical in nature, with strategic planning being the highest level and longest range form of planning. The same applies to information systems planning, though there does not necessarily have to be a one-for-one correspondence between the corporate planning hierarchy and that found most suitable for systems planning. Figure 2-7 suggests three possible levels of systems planning. The strategic plan deals with planning goals, the intermediate level plan with objectives and the lowest level plan with budgeting. Paralleling this planning structure, and related to it, are project plans which are initiated in furtherance of goals and objectives and which may extend from currently budgeted systems activities into the realm of intermediate planning with a three to five year horizon and even beyond into the long-range planning sector.

There are several implications in this layering of systems plans. First, different managerial groups are concerned with the preparation and review of plans at varying levels. The high level strategic plan is of principal interest to top management. The information systems steering committee, if one exists, would also be involved in evaluating and approving this plan.

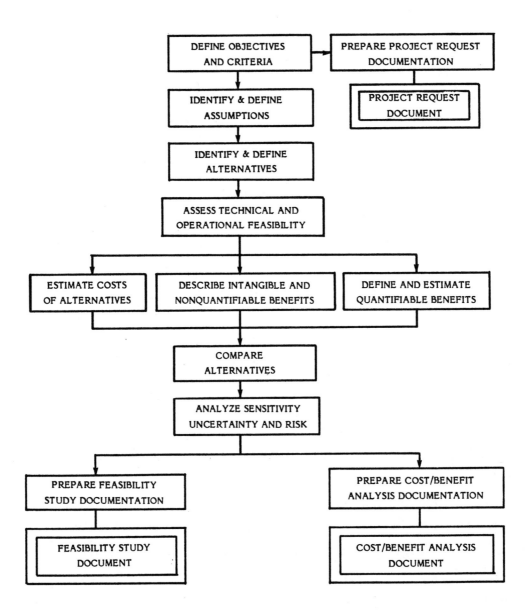

Figure 2-6/Key Activities of the Initiation Phase

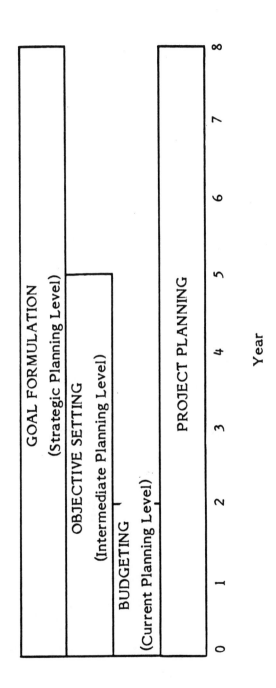

Figure 2-7/Levels of Systems Planning

Intermediate level plans concern primarily the director of information systems and other managers within the systems function who have responsibility for their accomplishment. An important factor in evaluating the performance of these managers should be their success in achieving planning objectives.

Budgetary planning involves systems managers as well as other levels of management responsible for approving proposed budgets. This may extend upward to top management in the case of proposals for large expenditures, such as a large capital investment for the purchase of data processing equipment.

Project planning may similarly involve several levels of management depending upon the estimated cost of the project. Below a certain level, perhaps $5,000 or $10,000, authorization of a new project may be discretionary with the director of information systems; at the other extreme, a proposed project with an estimated life cycle cost of several million dollars unquestionably should receive top management review before development proceeds. Within the federal government, large-scale projects receive different treatment from smaller projects both as to the methodology for their development and the review and approval steps associated with them. This methodology calls for mission analysis and consideration of alternative systems designs before full-scale development commitments can be made. If contractors are involved in the project, there could be parallel exploratory contracts before final contract award. Large scale projects of this kind require managerial responsibility to be placed at the level of a departmental assistant secretary.

Another distinguishing feature of the levels of systems planning is the degree of detail to be found in each type of plan. Because goal statements are nonquantitative, the strategic plan may be broad and contain little detail. At the intermediate level, objective statements should have associated with them quantitative data in the form of schedule milestones and resource requirements. And, of course, at the budgetary level there will be substantial detail covering systems expenditures by object class. Project plans may contain relatively gross estimates of cost, manpower and equipment requirements early in the initiation phase of the life cycle but should include very detailed estimates of these factors before the project is allowed to enter the development phase.

Controls over the implementation of planning goals and performance measurement of those charged with meeting them also vary according to the planning hierarchy. Top management should be concerned with the extent to which systems goals, along with other corporate goals, are being met. There should also be top management cognizance, at least on a management by exception basis, of the extent to which subordinate objectives are being accomplished in a timely and cost effective manner. The nature of budgetary control for information systems is similar to that for other functional areas, with managerial scrutiny and follow-up applied according to the principle of management by exception.

2.7 PLANNING IN A DECENTRALIZED ENVIRONMENT

Decentralization adds complexity to the planning process because it complicates the relationship between systems planning and corporate planning. Procedures for the various kinds of planning must provide guidance from headquarters to divisional managers, and divisional plans must be returned to headquarters for review and consolidation into an approved company-wide plan. To the extent that systems planning is tied into and subordinated to corporate planning, there must be feedback and interaction to assure that systems planners in the operating division prepare their plans in accordance not only with the overall corporate planning guidance but in furtherance of company-wide systems goals provided to them by the central systems staff. To avoid undue complexity, it may be desirable to delay the cycle for preparation of the systems plan until the corporate planning cycle has been completed.

If systems planning and budgeting are to be closely related, there is a similar need for coordination between the headquarters systems and budget staffs on the one hand and between them and their counterparts at the divisional level.

Project planning is a special case, since projects can be initiated at any time and have a life cycle that bears little relationship to annualized planning. Some method must be devised in a decentralized organization for communicating project plans from division to central staff prior to their initiation. We have mentioned dollar thresholds as a convenient way of permitting divisional autonomy and involving headquarters only in review of divisional project plans requiring significant resources.

If there is a well defined correspondence between company-wide systems goals and operating division goals, the problem of assuring that divisional project plans are consistent with company-wide goals is not so difficult. But where divisional systems planning goals and objectives are not documented, or where divisional systems plans are not subject to central coordination, staff review of project plans becomes critical and may indeed be the only means available for gaining divisional adherence to company-wide systems goals.

There are sometimes serious problems in trying to adapt the review of project plans to serve as a substitute for coordinating strategic planning by autonomous divisions. Divisional project planning may have progressed to a fairly detailed level before implementation costs are calculated and headquarters approval sought. By this time, potential systems users and divisional line management may be so committed to a project that it will be difficult to disapprove or redirect it.

The desirability of obtaining early warning about divisional project plans underscores the importance of life cycle management. If life cycle management procedures are applied, central staff planners can be apprised of project plans by means of documentation generated early in the initiation phase before much time and effort have been expended in a proposed new systems project.

2.8 CONVERSION PLANNING

In most organizations there exists today a large portfolio of applications that have been developed over many years. Some of these are undoubtedly candidates for upgrading or replacement, especially if they are programmed for obsolescent equipment. The portfolio of existing applications can impose serious constraints on systems planning by presenting problems of maintenance and conversion.

As the application portfolio expands over time, larger and larger proportions of total available resources must be devoted to maintenance. Systems analysts and programmers must spend an increasingly large amount of their time maintaining existing applications, with progressively less staff time available for development work. At the extreme, the systems staff may find itself so constrained by maintenance chores that it is unable to initiate desirable new projects without a staff increase or an augmentation of resources through contract programming.

The existing application portfolio often represents an investment of millions of dollars. If even a part of this investment is to be retained, a price must be paid to convert present applications to more sophisticated operating modes. Conversion problems typically arise in planning the transition from one model of computer to another, but these are by no means the only -- or even the most difficult -- conversion planning issues. Figure 2-8 shows a software prioritization table in which nine factors can be considered at any one of four levels. Each factor is also weighted and a value determined by multiplying the level by the weight. A total score can then be derived for each application being considered for conversion.

Major differences in design philosophy between old and new applications can be troublesome. For example, the conversion of an existing batch processing operation performed on a weekly cycle to a mode of immediate on-line transaction processing demands a whole new approach to data editing, file design and production of output reports. Similarly, the integration of "stand alone" applications such as accounts receivable, inventory control, accounts payable, payroll and general ledger into a single large system with common data elements would require a complete rework of existing applications.

A distinction should be made between straightforward application conversion and "resystemization" in planning the transition to a new equipment environment or from one application design philosophy to another and in estimating the cost of the transition. The simplest form of conversion is a line-for-line adaptation of a program or group of programs from one computer to another. This may or may not involve a change in programming language, e.g., assembly language to COBOL, or in equipment architecture, e.g., byte-oriented to word-oriented processing. The translation of computer programs with minimum change in the basic processing approach is fairly simple and can be costed with a higher degree of accuracy. (8)

SOFTWARE CONVERSION PRIORITIZATION

Factor Description \ Factor Level	1	2	3	4	Weighting Factor	Factor Level Value
1. Span of Operation	Infrequent use	Local	Multi unit	National/Multiagency		
2. Criticality	Critical to Single Project Operation	Critical to Routine Operation	Critical to Multiunit Operation	Critical to Multiagency Operation		
3. Development Cost	5K	5-15K	15-50K	Over 50K		
4. Maintenance Requirements	None	Very little	Heavy	Extensive		
5. Life Expectancy	1 year	1-2 years	3-5 years	Over 5 years		
6. System Complexity	Simple	Moderate	Difficult	Complex		
7. Change in Scope or Objectives	None	Infrequent	Occasional	Frequent or Continuous		
8. Number of Users	Very limited	Limited	Moderate	Extensive		
9. Personnel or Manpower Requirements	Very limited	Limited	Moderate	Extensive		
. . .	. . .	. . .	. . .	. . .		
					Factor Level Total	

Figure 2-8/Software Conversion Prioritization

Resystemization is undertaken when existing applications are so out of date that they are not worth considering for straight-line conversion. Here, essentially all or part of the application portfolio must be scheduled for replacement by completely redesigned new systems. The cost of paralleling new application development with maintenance of the old, and operating old and new equipment in parallel for months or even years, can be enormous and subject to large estimating errors.

Certain conditions may ease the burden of conversion, such as the prevalence of high level languages like COBOL and FORTRAN in the application portfolio or the replacement of one equipment configuration by another which possesses "upward compatibility." But ultimately a price must be paid to perpetuate existing applications or adapt them to future planning goals.

NOTES

1. Cyrus F. Gibson and Richard L. Nolan, "Managing the Four Stages of EDP Growth." Harvard Business Review, January-February, 1974; and Richard L. Nolan, "Managing Crises in Data Processing," Harvard Business Review, March-April, 1979.

2. For an expert presentation of the tenets of IRM, see Forest W. Horton, Jr., 'Information Resources Management: Concepts and Cases," Cleveland, Ohio, Association for Systems Management, 1979.

3. John T. Glennon, "Management Information Systems: The Role of Authority and Responsibility," MIS Quarterly, Volume 2, Number 2, June, 1978, p. 5.

4. See Frank R. Heath, "Guidelines for Identifying High Payoff Applications," Data Base, Volume 7, Number 3, Winter 1976, pp. 7-17. Also F. Warren McFarlan, "Portfolio Approach to Information Systems," Harvard Business Review, September-October, 1981, pp. 142-150.

5. Paul A. Strassman, "The Future Direction of Information Services to Impact the Bottom Line," Proceedings Eighth Annual Conference, Society for Management Information Systems, Chicago, September, 1976, pp. 37-46.

6. U.S. Department of Commerce, National Bureau of Standards, "Guidelines for Documentation of Computer Programs and Automated Data Systems," Federal Information Processing Standards Publication 38, Washington, U.S. Government Printing Office, February, 1976, pp. 6-7.

7. Executive Office of the President, Office of Management and Budget, Office of Federal Procurement Policy, "Major System Acquisitions," OFPP Pamphlet No. 1, August, 1976.

8. There are conversion aids in the form of translation programs which automatically convert from one programming language to another. Such conversion can be impeded, though, by the presence of program "patches" and lack of documentation typical of many older applications.

Chapter 3
The Methodology of Systems Planning

"Man is not the creature of circumstances;
circumstances are the creatures of men."

-- Benjamin Disraeli

An organization with little experience in systems planning has several approaches to consider in getting started. The quality and experience level of the professional staff is a major factor in determining the best way to proceed. As we have mentioned, there is no recognizable professional specialty concerned with systems planning, and so it is unlikely that technical staff members will possess directly relevant qualifications. There may, however, be staff members who have shown an affinity for planning, and this should certainly be exploited. A background in project planning and control, especially for large projects, can, for example, be adaptable to strategic planning. And staff members engaged in technology assessment, perhaps as a byproduct of evaluating equipment and software proposals or performing feasibility studies, may do well in a strategic planning assignment.

Qualifications of the technical staff is but one consideration. Of great practical importance is the availability of staff resources that can be devoted to planning. Some large firms are able to justify a specialized systems planning unit consisting of several professionals; in other cases, a single individual is given the assignment of coordinating the preparation of strategic plans, sometimes on a part-time basis. As a rule, at least two man-years are required to develop the initial version of a strategic plan, and it is unlikely that a plan can be adequately maintained without at least six man-months of effort per year.

An endorsement of strategic planning by top management, especially in the form of a written policy pronouncement, can assure that adequate staff resources are assigned to support the preparation and maintenance of plans. Preferably, this should take the form of a "charter" which spells out organizational and managerial responsibilities for planning.

3.1 INVOLVING TOP MANAGEMENT

Undoubtedly the most important principle of systems planning has to do with securing the active involvement of top management. This involvement should be sought at the inception of planning and should be maintained throughout the planning process. The involvement should have high visibility, such as could be demonstrated through participation by the company president in meetings of top officials devoted to initiating planning activity and reviewing planning progress.

Written evidence of top management interest, in the form of letters to officers and other managers, formalized policy statements and the like, can help reinforce the fact that top management regards systems planning as an important activity and expects subordinate managers to do likewise.

The Business Systems Planning (BSP) methodology of IBM provides a good example of an approach that stresses top management involvement. Under BSP, there is a "kickoff" meeting at the inception of planning. At this working session, which could take a half day to a full day or more, the chief executive meets with members of a planning task force who themselves are top company managers, preferably at the vice presidential level. Following this meeting the task force works full time for a minimum of eight weeks to produce the systems plan using a well-defined set of procedures. At the end of the BSP study, the chief executive once again meets with the task force to review recommendations and establish priorities.

In addition, BSP calls for a written statement issuance by the chief executive to be distributed at the kickoff meeting. This document stresses the importance the chief executive is attaching to the planning study.

3.2 ORGANIZING FOR PLANNING

There are three principal choices, not mutually exclusive, in launching a planning effort:

1. Activate a planning task force.

2. Prepare a staff written plan.

3. Bring in an outside consultant.

Let us consider each.

PLANNING TASK FORCE

There is considerable merit to convening a task force to draft an initial version of a strategic plan, especially in a diversified and decentralized organization in which it is important to get reliable inputs from operating divisions. Major organizational components and their needs can be reflected in the makeup of the task force. The task force approach can also draw upon the skills of senior people who could not be made available for a continuing full-time planning assignment.

In constituting a task force, it is desirable to seek a mixture of people with technical skills and those knowledgable about managerial and user requirements. If the task force is weighted too heavily with technical specialists, the resultant plan may not be meaningful to users. And the absence of sound technical thinking can lead to the positing of costly and unrealistic goals.

Systems professionals will ultimately be responsible for implemeneting most planning goals. Users of computer services must rely on information systems to carry out their own goals within engineering, marketing, manufacturing and elsewhere throughout the organization. It is, therefore, beneficial to combine these two perspectives in a planning task force, recognizing that the resultant grouping may be burdened by the well known difficulty of technicians and line managers in communicating with each other. To avoid this communications gap, the task force could be directed to concentrate on identifying user goals and requirements, with the systems specialist's role restricted to providing workload projections and indicating technological constraints.

If the organization is decentralized to the extent that significant systems capability exists within line operating divisions, it may be desirable to invite senior professionals from each operating unit to serve on the task force with corporate systems planners. In this way, division representatives could play a dual role by contributing to the technical portions of the plan while at the same time representing the requirements and interests of their parent division.

One difficult problem for those representing operating divisions, regardless of whether or not they have a computer background, is in adopting an organization-wide perspective in formulating planning goals. As task force members, they must condition their thinking to avoid unduly furthering the interests of a particular division in resource allocation decisions. Such parochialism must be minimized if an optimum company-wide plan is to be produced.

The size of a planning task force can, of course, vary according to the scope and diversity of company oeprations, but it should be held within manageable bounds. A group of more than a dozen becomes unwieldly and inhibits close personal interaction among task force members. If there are a large number of operating units, it is better to select task force members from among these units, perhaps on the basis of technical sophistication, rather than simply allocating one member per unit to participate. Besides limiting its size, those organizing the task force should exercise "quality control" to assure that those named have the personal potential to make a contribution.

Because the planning task force will deal with broad goals and issues, it should be able to complete its work within a fairly limited time, leaving detailed implementation planning to others. In several instances, a strategic planning exercise has been completed within a single week, and it is not unreasonable to expect results from a planning task force with a month or two.

The productivity of the task force depends not just on careful selection of its members; it hinges equally on the working environment provided and the extent of advance preparation. Task force members should be isolated from their normal working environment, preferably away from a company facility. A remote location in which outside distractions are limited permits the most productive use of time and encourages informal discussion of issues after hours. One successful planning session was held at a small dude ranch in Arizona where outside telephone communication was restricted.

Advance staff work by systems specialists can help assure a productive task force session. Background papers can be provided covering such matters as the history of data processing within the company, equipment and application profiles and workload projections. For task force members who are not computer specialists, it is useful to arrange a briefing at the opening session to survey the state-of-the-art in equipment, software and data communications.

Written materials should be distributed to task force members in advance of their working sessions. The meetings themselves should be structured, not to the point of inhibiting creativity but to assure that the group will not simply disperse after a week of interesting conversation without producing a tangible end product. This implies a strong task force leader, an agenda of topics to be covered and a checklist of items to be produced. The output of the group should be documented, at least in rough draft form, before it adjourns and its members return to day-to-day operating concerns. This should be mandatory even though it may require secretarial support at the meeting site.

STAFF WRITTEN PLANS

Staff prepared plans drafted within the information systems function have the advantage of being more amenable to control than those of task forces in terms of quality, scope of coverage and preparation schedule. There must, of course, be available adequate skills to produce a draft plan either as an ad hoc assignment or through creation of a full-time planning staff.

Because of the importance of user involvement, a staff prepared plan should be based upon user requirements analysis. The draft plan should be circulated to users for review before final issuance or submission to the systems steering committee. A staff prepared plan could, indeed, serve as input to a planning task force consisting of user representatives convened to review and modify its contents.

Some authorities hold that it is not essential, and may even be undesirable, to have plans originated by the information systems function. They argue that there is merit in divorcing systems planning from those who have the responsibility for implementation. By making this separation, the organization may achieve greater objectivity in formulating planning goals and find it easier to gain the understanding and approval of top management. It may also avoid the possible diversion of resources to projects that are technically interesting but have a relatively low priority in management's scheme of things.

Some companies have detached systems planning from other information systems activities by creating a systems planning unit within the corporate planning staff. (2) This has the advantage of giving information system plans the specialized attention they require while avoiding conflicts of interest and exposing systems planners to a corporate-wide perspective.

CONSULTANTS

Use of consultants in preparing a strategic plan offers the usual benefits associated with consulting: the acquisition of specialized skills not available within the organization and assurance of objectivity in formulating goals and objectives. Because information systems planning is a relatively new and uncharted field, it is not easy to find consultants with established planning credentials. A common pitfall to be avoided lies in confusing experience in project planning with the expertise needed for strategic planning. As we have noted, there is abundant experience available in planning and controlling individual systems development projects, but the concepts and techniques of project management are inadequate for devising a sound strategic plan.

Consulting experience in corporate planning may be transferable to the information systems area. The danger here is that technical capabilities, and risks, may be poorly understood and superficially evaluated with a resultant lack of realism in formulating systems goals.

Regardless of the approach chosen to get started, the planning process should be formalized and documented through written procedures, forms, policy statements and schedules of events for preparation, review, and publication of the plan. Equally desirable is the designation of a unit or an individual as having systems planning responsibility. In organizations that do not have the resources to assign a full-time staff to systems planning, someone should still be designated as the focal point for planning activity. Unless at least half the time of a senior staff member can be devoted to planning, it is probably not worthwhile to try to maintain a standing plan. Sometimes, planning responsibility can be combined with related functions to justify a full-time position. For example, systems planning could be allied with research into the applicability of new equipment and software.

3.3 DATA COLLECTION

The systems planning process must be strengthened and supported by the availability of specific details concerning present capabilities. Such data collection requires careful preparatory work prior to drafting the plan itself.

There is need for an inventory of what is on hand in the way of systems resources: equipment, software, personnel and dollars. Compiling such an inventory may seem like an obvious first step, but in a decentralized operating environment, where resources are not acquired and controlled by the central staff, it can be no small problem to determine just what capabilities are presently available.

EQUIPMENT

It is useful, not only for plannning but for other purposes, to maintain an equipment inventory, including not just computers -- large and small -- but front-end processors, microprocessors, terminals and data communications equipment. Inventory records should contain a description of equipment capability and capacity, an indication of physical location, whether the equipment is owned or rented, and other data that could be helpful in evaluating the adequacy of existing equipment resources. Figure 3-1 gives an indication of the items of information that are maintained by one large organization.

This should be considered the minimum compilation of data on equipment resources. Figure 3-2 shows a worksheet for obtaining information regarding the usage to which the equipment is being devoted. Often, such information can be obtained as a by-product of the chargeback system for computer services.

SOFTWARE

It is also helpful to prepare an inventory of software capability, in the form of descriptions of the existing application portfolio. The inventory should identify the nature and size of each application, its technical characteristics such as programming language and computer configuration and its periodicity of operation. Figure 3-3 provides a checklist of application characteristics that could usefully be maintained in an application inventory.

Besides collecting this basic information about the application portfolio, it is desirable to undertake an analysis of the adequacy of existing systems, along the lines depicted in Figure 3-4. Similarly, a review of the status of applications under development, as shown in Figure 3-5, can provide valuable insight into what resources have already been committed and for how long.

Because such data collection efforts can be time consuming and costly, they should be restricted to the larger and more significant applications and projects which account for the preponderance of software resources.

PERSONNEL

In assessing the present state of systems capability as the basis for developing realistic plans, a review of human resources available to implement plans should be made. Figure 3-6 shows one example of a personnel summary.

If planning objectives are to be tempered with realism, the strengths and limitations of the staff available to accomplish them must be taken into account.

1.   Reporting Unit Code

2.   Class of Equipment Code

3.   Equipment Name, e.g., CPU, Disk Unit

4.   Manufacturer Name

5.   Manufacturer Type Number

6.   Manufacturer Model Number

7.   Manufacturer Serial Number

8.   Date of Acquisition

9.   Date of Purchase

10.   Purchase Price

11.   Rental Cost

12.   Maintenance Cost

13.   Date Reported

Figure 3-1/Equipment Inventory Data Elements

Reporting Unit: Period Covered: Date:

Average Monthly Computer Resource

Function   Units or Estimated Cost

1. Finance/Accounting

2. Marketing

3. Manufacturing

4. Research/Engineering

5. Administration

6. Personnel

7. Internal (Program test, etc.)

8. Systems/Technical Support

9. Other (Specify)

Figure 3-2/Distribution of Computer Resources

1.   Reporting Unit Code

2.   Application Type, e.g., Scientific, Administrative

3.   Application Name

4.   Application Status, e.g., Planned, Operational

5.   Programming Language

6.   Processing Environment, e.g., Local Batch, Remote Batch

7.   Processing Equipment, e.g., IBM 370-168

8.   Implementation Date (Planned or Actual)

9.   Narrative Abstract

10.   Date Reported

Figure 3-3/Application Inventory Data Elements

A. APPLICATION DESCRIPTION

   1.   Name of system:

   2.   User department:

   3.   Frequency of runs:

   4.   Type of system (interactive, batch, etc.):

   5.   Planning, control or operational function:

   6.   Year originally started: Year put into production:

   7.   Current annual operating cost

       a.   Information Services cost:

       b.   User cost:

   8.   Volumes of transactions going through system:

B. ASSESSMENT OF THE APPLICATION

   1.   Original intent of the system:

   2.   What it actually does, and its impact on user areas:

   3.   Benefits derived from the system:

   4.   Outstanding problem areas

       a.   User perspective:

       b.   Information Services perspective:

   5.   Adequacy of documentation

       a.   Are user procedures developed such that only limited training is required for new personnel?

       b.   Is user documentation current?

       c.   Is the system and program documentation current?

       d.   Is extensive training required for analysts and programmers before they can be effective in the system?

C. CURRENTLY IDENTIFIED PLANS

   1.   Life expectancy of the system:

   2.   Brief description of major changes or enhancements:

   3.   Need for a rewrite or redesign:

   4.   Cost of identified plans:

   5.   Level of ongoing effort

       a.   modification, enhancements:

       b.   maintenance:

   6.   Cost of

       a.   modification:

       b.   maintenance:

Figure 3-4/Assessment of Current Applications

A. PROJECT DESCRIPTION

     1.   Reporting Unit: Date:

     2.   Project Number: Project Name:

     3.   Purpose of Project:

     4.   General Description:

B. DEVELOPMENT EFFORT

     1.   Design/Programming expended to _____ $ _____ M/M _____
                                            (date)

     2.   Testing expended to _____ $ _____ HRS _____
                                     (date)

     3.   Other Costs (itemize) expended to _____ $ _____
                                          (date)

C. OPERATIONAL REQUIREMENTS

     1.   Forecasted Annual Computer Use

           Upon Completion $ _____

     2.   Estimated Annual Maintenance Costs $ _____ M/M _____

     3.   Other Costs (itemize) $ _____

D. ANNUAL BENEFITS

     1.   Tangible   _____   _____   _____
                       Headcount $ Other $ Total $

     2.   Intangible (describe)

Figure 3-5/Analysis of Ongoing Projects

Reporting Unit: Date:

Job Category	Actual 19__ Filled	Actual 19__ Vacant	Current Year Budget	Forecasts 19__	19__
1. Management					
2. Supervisor					
3. Consultant/Project Leader					
4. Analyst					
5. Analyst/Programmer or Programmer					
6. OR/MS Analyst					
7. Systems Programmer					
8. Data Entry Operator					
9. Data Comm. Operator					
10. Computer Operator					
11. Services & Support					
12. Methods & Procedures Analyst					
13. Other (Identify by title/definition)					

Figure 3-6/Personnel Summary

Otherwise, objectives will not be achieved or will require a personnel increase unacceptable to management.

An appraisal of human resources should consider not just the headcount but the capabilities of both professional staff members and the systems management team. If the professional staff is too heavily committed or lacks the technical skills needed for advanced application development, plans must be made for augmentation through stepped-up recruiting or the use of outside contractors. Managerial deficiencies, especially in project planning and control, are not so easily remedied.

Whatever the level and quality of available personnel, their productivity can be enhanced through the discipline of a strong standards program and through the application of formalized project control procedures that identify delays and critical development problems in time for early remedial action.

COSTS

A careful analysis of current and projected costs attributable to information systems should be undertaken as a prelude to planning. This can be done fairly easily if there are: 1) project control procedures that permit the distribution of costs by project, 2) chargeback mechanisms to distribute both application development and computer center operating costs among end users. Where there are no cost accounting methods for information systems, a special effort will have to be made to identify such costs. Figure 3-7 indicates the cost categories covered in a typical cost analysis.

At the inception of planning, some indication should be sought from top management as to spending constraints that should be applied in formulating plans. Is it management's desire that systems costs be held constant, or even reduced, over the next few years? Or will increase be permitted only to the extent needed to handle a growth in workload volumes? (3)

Where planning constraints permit only limited expansions of systems resources, existing cost components should be analyzed to determine whether a reallocation

1. <u>Capital Investments ($000)</u>   <u>FY__</u>   <u>FY__</u>   <u>FY__</u>
                                                        (actual)   (actual)   (estimated)

    A.   Purchase of new capacity

    B.   Purchases to expand or replace existing capacity

    C.   Purchase of software

    D.   Site

              Subtotal

2. <u>Personnel ($000)</u>

    A.   Compensation and benefits

    B.   Travel

3. <u>Equipment Rental, Space and Other Operating Costs ($000)</u>

    A.   Rentals

    B.   Space

    C.   Supplies and Other

              Subtotal

4. <u>Outside Services ($000)</u>

    A.   Time Sharing

    B.   Software Packages

    C.   Systems Analysis and Programming

    D.   Maintenance

    E.   Consulting

              Subtotal

Figure 3-7/Current and Projected Costs

of costs would free resources for work on planning objectives. Conversion of existing applications to newer equipment might offer opportunities for reductions in operating and maintenance costs, for example. Reassignment of analysts and programmers from low priority projects in one user area to implement more critical planning objectives is another possibility. In the past, consolidation of computer facilities to achieve economies of scale has shown impressive cost savings in many organizations.

3.4 MANAGERIAL AND USER REQUIREMENTS

Besides surveying existing resources, an analysis must be made to determine future managerial requirements for information systems and to identify user needs. The distinction between managerial and user requirements is made in recognition of the special needs of managers, especially top management and the managers of major operating divisions, for systems support. User requirements analysis addresses the needs of those responsible for conducting day-to-day operations.

It is to be hoped that, after surveying both kinds of requirements, there will be large areas of overlap in demand for new computer services. If, for example, marketing management desires more sophisticated tools for sales forecasting, this may tie in with an equivalent demand for improvement in lower level applications for order entry, accounts receivable and sales analysis.

MANAGEMENT INFORMATION SYSTEMS

Specialists in the design of information systems are wont to comment on the difficulty of performing requirements analysis to ascertain management's information needs. Some have devised elaborate techniques involving structured interviews, questionnaires and similar methods to obtain an indication of these information needs. Others point out the drawbacks of such techniques, asserting that managerial problem solving is "ad hoc" in nature and that management's information needs cannot be anticipated in advance by systems designers. They note that much of top management's decision making has a one-time characteristic, such as selection of a new plant location or the introduction of a new product line. They note further the danger of structuring application and data base design to reflect the interests and proclivities of a particular executive who will eventually be replaced by a successor who may have entirely different information requirements. This has been discussed in terms of information "thresholds." One manager may be a "detail" man, seeking significant amounts of quantitative data concerning the decision at hand while another may desire only the "big picture" by means of summaries and salient facts affecting a decision. (4)

Some authorities are confident that the role of the computer in supporting managerial decision making will be expanded. Simon, for instance, is optimistic that programmed kinds of decisions will be gradually extended upward within the management hierarchy. (5) And Gibson and Nolan believe that the integrated systems produced during stage four of EDP growth will provide more relevant computer based information to management. (6)

Some who question the efficacy of investing extensive effort in requirements analysis for management information do not dispute the potentially important role of the computer in supporting managerial decision making. They argue instead for greater flexibility in system design to permit managers to call for items of information when they are needed. The methodology of contemporary data base design is consistent with this viewpoint. By means of multiple indexes and pointers, online inquiries can be made of data bases in direct access storage to permit selective retrieval of desired information. And interactive querying and computer assisted problem solving can be facilitated by nontechnical query languages and parameterized models that do not require the specialized talents of computer programmers in their usage.

In most situations, there is a rational middle ground between seeking a definitive statement of managerial information requirements on the one hand and foregoing an attempt to design information systems to support managerial decision making on the other. Some information is known to have value, such as reports to the top management of an airline on the load factor, i.e., number of passengers carried during each day's operation, or advance passenger bookings. Where such requirements are readily identified, systems plans can be drawn up to better support these managerial needs, either through the development of new applications or the improvement of existing ones to provide information in more timely and understandable fashion. In this category would be efforts to convert from cyclical to on-line processing and to provide graphic output in place of tabular reports.

Regardless of the enthusiasm of top management for computer technology, their information needs must be considered in formulating the strategic plan. In one situation they may be only a minor component of the final plan; in another they may be deemed of critical importance.

USER REQUIREMENTS ANALYSIS

Beyond considering managerial requirements, the needs of other users of information services must be taken into account. The user community in an organization can range from large operating divisions, for which major applications must be developed, to individual users like research scientists and engineers. An up-to-date application inventory is a good starting point for undertaking a survey of user requirements.

Figure 3-8 shows an example of a planning form tied into the life cycle management concepts previously discussed. It identifies planned applications both in their initiation and their development phases. As an application progresses from initiation to development, the form is resubmitted to show additional detail.

The type of user survey that may turn out to be most beneficial in systems planning, and the amount of effort devoted to such a survey, depend largely upon the kind of organization structure in which new applications are authorized and developed. In a centralized information systems activity, in which a central staff provides operational computer services and undertakes new application development projects in response to user requests, the identification of existing and future application needs will be easier than in a decentralized organization in which users have their own technical staff resources and budgets as well as authority to initiate new projects without prior approval. In one such organization a consultant had to be retained at a cost of more than $100,000 to catalogue existing and planned applications and set up an automated data base of application

I. Application Initiation			
Reporting Unit	Date	Application Type	Application Name

Narrative

Summary of Benefits		Date	Processing Cycle

	Management Approval		☐ One Time
			☐ Random
			☐ Scheduled
			  Frequency _____
			  (Specify)

	Cost Benefit		

Schedule Dates	Cost Estimates	Processing Environment
Design _____ Programming_____ Operation	Development Phase _____ Dollars _____ % Outside _____ Operation Phase	☐ On-Line ☐ Local Batch ☐ Remote Batch

Planned Processing Center In-House _____ Other *(Specify)*	Application Status ☐ New ☐ Conv. ☐ Redesign	Application Development ☐ In-House ☐ Outside

Security ☐ Yes ☐ No	Personal Data ☐ Yes ☐ No	Application Type	DBMS Application ☐ Yes ☐ No	Mission Critical ☐ Yes ☐ No

II. Application Development			
Development Phase Definition	Schedule Dates	Cost Estimate	Man-Years
Design			
Programming			
Test			
Operation Phase			

Number of Application Subsystems	Test Plan ☐ Yes ☐ No	Parallel OPR ☐ Yes ☐ No	Storage Media	Transaction Volume	File Size

Terminal Requirements	Remote Job Entry (RJE)		Interactive		Dual
	Intelligent	Non-Intelligent	Intelligent	Non-Intelligent	
Currently Available					
Acquisition Planned					
Total ⟶					

Special Needs	Equipment	Software

Possible Common Use ☐ Yes ☐ No	Programming Language ☐ COBOL ☐ FORTRAN ☐ Other *(Specify)*

Figure 3-8/Application Planning Form

information. (7)

One pitfall in performing user requirements analysis is that it may produce an extended "wish list" of applications, many of which fall into the desirable rather than essential category. This is especially likely when there is no charge-back mechanism to discipline user demands for new applications to be developed by a central systems staff. As has been mentioned in the context of project planning, it is usually necessary to assign priorities to application plans once the requirements analysis is completed. Regardless of the extent to which user requirements are eventually translated into approved planning objectives, there is merit in determining potential needs for computer services as an input to the strategic planning process.

3.5 PROJECTING DEMAND FOR SERVICES

Besides analysis of managerial and user requirements, insight can be gained into the probable scope of future systems activities through extrapolations of past operating experience. Where an existing application or group of applications has been automated for several years, reasonably accurate projections of future growth in transaction processing volumes, file sizes and other characteristics can be made. These can then be transformed into equipment capacity requirements.

Projections can similarly be made in a computer service center environment based not on the growth of particular applications but on statistics as to the numbers and types of jobs processed during a given period. Figure 3-9 charts the workload of one large multicenter operation in terms of thousands of jobs per month over an eight-year period.

Reliance on projections in estimating future processing volumes and gauging user demand has the serious deficiency attributable to any straight-line extrapolation. A change in technology, such as the shift that is now taking place away from centralized facilities toward data networks and distributed processing, can trigger significant increases in user demand for services and foster the development of new applications as well as the adaptation of existing applications. This can result in major perturbations not only in the volume of work to be done, but in the

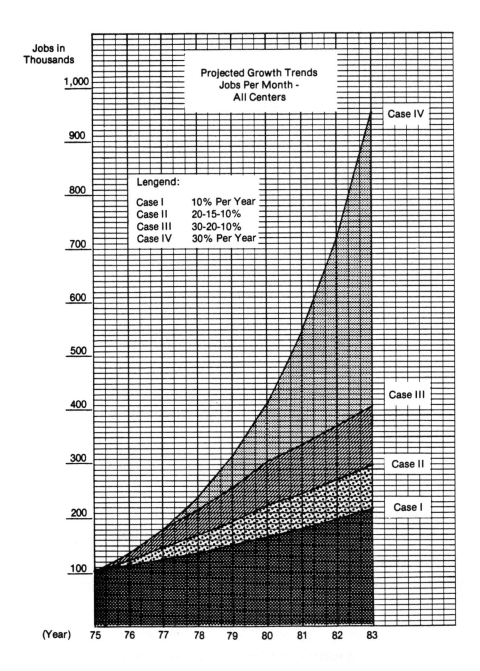

Figure 3-9/Workload Projection

location at which such work is to be performed. There could, for example, be an increase in processing workloads on minicomputers at remote locations accompanied by a leveling off or decrease in throughput at large central processing sites.

The impact of technology is but one factor that can distort workload projections. A drastic change in business operations, such as new product introductions or mergers and acquisitions, can affect the accuracy of projections. In the public sector, new legislation affecting social security assistance payments or changing food stamp eligibility requirements can have an equally distorting impact. (8)

3.6 TECHNOLOGY ASSESSMENT

We have just noted the drawbacks of projections of workload and equipment usage as a basis for strategic planning. There is a body of more sophisticated techniques that has come to be collectively described by such terms as "technology assessment" or "technology forecasting." Technology assessment undertakes to predict the future characteristics and impact of technology. Assessments have been made in many fields over the past few years, covering such diverse subjects as agricultural production, energy resources and transportation. Assessments also have been made of computer technology -- the principal area of concern to information systems planners.

There are interesting differences of opinion as to whether futurists, armed with outputs of technology assessment, can use these as means of actually controlling future events. A charge sometimes leveled at the technological forecaster is that "you can't predict a breakthrough." But this may not necessarily be so. It is possible to predict a future increase, say, in productivity within a given industry based on the probable invention of a labor-saving device without actually identifying the particular invention that may cause the breakthrough to higher productivity levels. For purposes of planning, it is often sufficient to predict that innovation will take place, without pinpointing the precise nature of the change.

Technology assessment can be distinguished from mere speculation about the future in two respects. First, it is conducted through the application of a disciplined methodology; and, second, it seeks to provide information of significance to those directly concerned with planning.

As one futurist has noted, the principal difference between technology assessment and speculation lies "in the attempts on the part of the forecaster to achieve precision in the description of the useful machine whose characteristics he is forecasting and in his attempts to place the forecast on a sound scientific foundation through the use of logical and explicit methods. A well done forecast will state the predicted characteristics of the machine being forecast and make clear the means by which the forecast was arrived at." (9)

In contrast to intuitive forecasting of the kind derived by "asking an expert," the methodology of technology assessment embraces the following general approaches.

SOPHISTICATED EXTRAPOLATION

There are a variety of methods for attempting to overcome the deficiencies of straightforward projections. Trend extrapolation attempts to relate the projected development or performance of several phenomena that have similar characteristics rather than considering only a single phenomenon. For example, projection of future demand for computer center services might be associated with sales forecasts made by the marketing department or with external projections of growth in other segments of computer technology such as timesharing.

"Envelope" curves can be derived to produce extrapolations which show variations in growth of demand for computer resources, with an indication of the probability that a straightforward projection will either be exceeded or fail to be achieved. Such projections have been used in deriving workload estimates as a basis for government computer procurements. This provides prospective bidders with an indication of the maximum and minimum commitment of the customer to augment an initial equipment configuration over the duration of the contract period.

Regardless of the degree of refinement embodied in statistical projections, extrapolations remain tied to the basic limiting assumption "that the conditions that prevailed in the past and were responsible for the well behaved trend observed in the data will continue unchanged into the future, at least as far as the time of the desired prediction. No amount of mathematical sophistication in treatment of the data can make up for the breakdown of this assumption." (10)

CONSENSUS METHODS

The opinions of an expert have always been of value in technology assessment. Consensus methods of assessment seek to overcome the drawbacks of relying on the predictions of a single expert by broadening the base of expert opinion and focusing the efforts of these experts by means of specific forecasting methodology. The most widely used consensus method is the Delphi technique which obtains the opinions of a panel of experts through a series of questionnaires. In the first questionnaire, the respondents, who are not identified to each other in advance, are asked to make a forecast by replying to a series of questions about future technology. The replies are combined into a composite forecast which shows the extent of differences of opinion among the respondents as to the likelihood and the time of occurrence of a particular event. This is followed by a second questionnaire which asks each panelist to react to the composite forecast by either modifying his earlier response or stating reasons why he continues to disagree with the composite result. This process is continued through subsequent questionnaires in an effort to achieve convergence.

The Delphi method offers significant advantages over intuitive forecasts by committees of experts. The anonymity provided makes it easier for the experts to consider arguments on their merits without being influenced by the presence or personal opinions of others. Similary, respondents can more easily abandon previous positions without loss of face if they become convinced that earlier positions at variance with the composite forecast were erroneous. Usually, three rounds of questionnaires are required for the panelists to achieve convergency in making a prediction.

SIMULATION

Simulation, usually aided by computerized mathematical models, endeavors to explicitly identify key functional elements in the technology under consideration and to express the relationships among these elements. These relationships determine the rate at which progress in some aspect of technology can be expected to be achieved. There are many simulation models and methods that are adaptable to technology assessment.

Cross impact analysis is based upon an analytical model of a set of probable future events. Its unique strength lies in its ability to deal quantitatively with interdependencies among events. As shown in Figure 3-10, having to do with weather forecasting, the probability of occurrence of each event is first predicted and subsequently modified based upon the probability of occurrence of the other events. This permits computer modeling in which an event is selected at random based on its probability of occurrence, with subsequent adjustment of the probability of the remaining events according to the cross impact matrix. A second event can then be randomly selected from among those remaining with the cross impact calculations continuing until all events in the set have been decided. (11)

3.7 EPISODIC VERSUS ANNUALIZED PLANNING

Many organizations venturing into systems planning for the first time tacitly assume that their plans should be updated annually. This is a convenient assumption when systems planning is tied to an annual corporate planning process or when such planning is related to a yearly budget preparation cycle. But performing systems planning on an annual basis may be merely an administrative convenience and not necessarily represent the best utilization of planning resources. Ackoff points out that "planning should be a continuous process and hence no plan is ever final; it is always subject to revision. A plan therefore is not the final product of the planning process: it is an interim report." (12)

Because the strategic plan deals with broad goals for the development of information systems, it is unlikely that these goals, once articulated initially, will change markedly in the course of a single year. For this reason, "ad hoc" or

If This Event Were To Occur	Having Had This Probability of Occurrence by 1985	Then the Probability of This Event Also Occurring Would Become			
		A	B	C	D
A. One-Month Reliable Weather Forecasts	0.4		0.2 (Same)	0.5 (Same)	0.7 (Higher)
B. Feasibility of Limited Weather Control	0.2	0.5 (Higher)		0.5 (Same)	0.65 (Higher)
C. General Biochemical Immunization	0.5	0.4 (Same)	0.2 (Same)		0.5 (Same)
D. Elimination of Crop Damage From Adverse Weather	0.5	0.4 (Same)	0.2 (Same)	0.5 (Same)	

Figure 3-10/Cross Impact Matrix

episodic planning may prove suitable, in which the plan is reviewed and updated whenever events dictate major changes in strategic goals.

If an annual cycle is not adhered to, the planning staff should monitor the state of technology, corporate goals and environmental factors and initiate action to revise the plan whenever circumstances change significantly. A reorganization, for example, might trigger an extensive revision of the plan to reflect changing company goals. Or a major technological development, such as the acquisition of a sohisticated new computer, could engender significant changes in user demand patterns that must be responded to by the systems staff. Given the volatile state of computer technology, the plan probably should be revised at least every three years even if there is no major external occurrence or internal policy shift that dictates a revision.

A comprehensive method of maintaining currency in the strategic plan is to issue a basic planning document initially and supplement it annually with new material, such as updated projections of data processing workloads or revised objectives based on newly identified user requirements. Other parts of the plan would be revised only when needed. A loose leaf notebook format is suitable in these circumstances, with some sections of the plan remaining intact and others re-placed each year.

The choice between episodic and annualized planning has been summarized by McFarlan:

> Given the great difficulty of EDP planning, should one put together an
> EDP plan on a regular basis or rather, as some organizations have done,
> only every two to four years? The idea behind the latter alternative is
> to try to do the job right once, and then make only minor updates for
> the next couple of years. (13)

It is a choice that should be weighed carefully by systems planners before commit-ting their organization to the burden of maintaining an annual plan.

NOTES

1. Alan C. Stanford, "How to Maintain Top Management Interest in the Plan," Proceedings Tenth Annual Conference, Society for Management Information Systems, Washington, September, 1978.

2. William Woodside, "A View from the Top," Proceedings Tenth Annual Conference, Society for Management Information Systems, Washington, September, 1978. The views of Mr. Woodside, President of American Can Company, are of particular interest because of his earlier background in planning and systems analysis.

3. If each new large-scale application development project must be subjected to rigorous cost-benefit analysis before it gains management approval, there is less need to involve top management closely in reviewing preliminary cost projections made in conjunction with systems planning. Management will have an opportunity later to review the cost impact of each new project proposal.

4. Head, pp. 34-36.

5. Simon, pp. 30-32.

6. Gibson and Nolan, pp. 86-87.

7. There are numerous guidelines available that provide forms and procedures for conducting a requirements analysis. IBM's Business Systems Planning (BSP) approach, which organizes planning into five well defined phases, has been used successfully in both commercial and public organizations. Business Systems Planning, IBM Corporation, Technical Publications/Industry, Dept. 825, White Plains, N.Y., August, 1975.

8. It is common in conducting equipment procurements in public agencies to attempt to quantify workloads over a five to eight year period to provide

prospective bidders with a basis for sizing and configuring proposed equipment. This constitutes planning of a sort but suffers from the same deficiencies as other forms of straight-line workload projections.

9.   Joseph P. Martino, "An Introduction to Technological Forecasting," Gordon and Breach Science Publishers, New York, 1972, p. 13.

10.   Op. cit., p. 21.

11.   Table 3-10 is drawn from materials in the Conference Notebook of the Future Research Techniques Conference for Corporate Planners, Center for Management Education, Graduate School of Business, University of Southern California, April, 1976.

12.   Ackoff, p. 5.

13.   F. Warren McFarlan, "Planning the Information Function," Proceedings Eighth Annual Conference, Society for Management Information Systems, Chicago, September, 1976, p. 64.

Chapter 4
Practicalities in Systems Planning

"The perfect is the enemy of the good."

-- John B. Medaris

Few executives would quarrel with the concept of formalized planning as a means of improving organizational effectiveness. Yet in practice planning is often neglected or viewed as a luxury, expendable during a profit crunch or organizational retrenchment. This is the case not only with systems planning but with other kinds of long-range planning.

Even without strong managerial support, bottom-up planning can be undertaken. But there must be at least a minimum commitment on the part of management. Strong top management endorsement of planning is vital, especially in a decentralized organization in which line operating divisions must contribute to the formulation of organization-wide plans. There must be assurance from management that adequate resources will be applied to planning throughout the organization. And this must be backed up by policies and procedures supporting preparation and review of plans.

The concepts underlying strategic planning -- whether corporate-wide or specifically for information systems -- are not difficult to grasp. The methodology of planning is now sufficiently well established that it can readily be applied in organizations willing to make a commitment to planning. But there remain practical problems that inhibit effective planning. In this chapter, we shall deal with some of these and offer suggestions for doing a more effective planning job.

4.1 DETERRENTS TO EFFECTIVE PLANNING

Unless there is a good climate for systems planning, it may be better for the systems staff _not_ to undertake strategic planning but to concentrate instead on more immediate objectives that are acceptable to management. Among the chief problems that can hamper the conduct of systems planning are the following.

INABILITY TO GAIN MANAGERIAL INVOLVEMENT AND SUPPORT

Because planning requires the diversion of manpower and other scarce resources from more immediate tasks, and imposes constraints and disciplines on line managers that they sometimes view as inimical to their short run interests, lack of top management support can be a serious, even fatal, weakness in performing systems planning. Managerial support is needed not just in getting started but in following up to measure adherence to plans.

The absence of top management support is not necessarily an indictment of the short sightedness of policy level managers; it may reflect equally on the systems staff for a failure to sell top management on the benefits of planning and to relate the importance of systems support to the broader goals of the organization. From the infancy of business data processing, much has been said about the "communications gap" between computer professionals and others in the organization. Initiatives to breach this gap are vital in the area of systems planning which has the potential to provide a crucial linkage between top management and the systems function.

FAILURE TO REVIEW PLANS

As an integral part of the planning process there must be managerial review to assure that plans are not merely formulated and submitted but are followed in a practical way in managerial decision making. There may be some benefit in initiating systems planning and producing a strategic plan even if there is not adequate followup with top management. But the planning cycle is incomplete unless there is a meaningful review of plans by management, with feedback to the systems staff in the form of deletions, additions or changes to planning goals and objectives.

It is open to question whether the systems plan should be presented to top management in preliminary form or withheld until a fairly complete set of plans has been produced. The benefit of early interaction is that guidance can be received concerning goals, assumptions and constraints, especially with regard to availability of resources for planned expansions of systems activities. On the other hand, if an incomplete and poorly justified plan is submitted, there may be a negative reaction on the part of management to newly proposed goals and objectives.

If management objects to "surprises," the plan should certainly be presented while in its formative stages. And if management has a genuine interest in systems planning, and is willing to contribute to improving the plan, early involvement is bound to be productive.

LACK OF PLANNING DIRECTIVES AND PROCEDURES

To do all but the most casual kind of planning, there must be carefully thought out policies and procedures which delineate responsibilities for planning, the scope of planning, the methodology to be employed, the planning cycle and review and control requirements. Without such guidelines for preparation and documentation of plans, there can be little quality control over the final product. In a decentralized environment, procedures are essential if there is to be consistency among division plans which must be consolidated into a company-wide plan.

Where there are well defined corporate planning procedures, it is easier to develop information systems planning as an adjunct to corporate planning. If corporate planning has not been formalized, the task of initiating systems planning and gaining acceptance of planning goals and objectives becomes more difficult.

INSUFFICIENT ALLOCATION OF RESOURCES TO PLANNING

The resource commitment for planning varies, of course, with the size of the organization and with the degree to which it is computer intensive. Moreover, the visibility of planning resources may be greater where planning activity is centralized rather than distributed among several operating divisions. Though there are few rules of thumb to indicate the minimum resources required, there must be a dual commitment of: 1) adequate staff time for planning, and 2) managerial time for review and followup. Once the planning process has been initiated and the initial plan produced, the staff required to maintain the plan is usually less than that required for initiation. (1)

It is evident that these deterrents are interrelated, with the likelihood that if one deficiency is present, it will be accompanied by others. It is also apparent that a crucial factor in effective systems planning is to relate it to other planning activities in which top management is already involved and which already have solid support. This argues strongly for establishing a linkage between systems planning and corporate planning and annual budget operating plan preparation.

4.2 CONTROL MECHANISMS

If the goal statements embodied in the information systems plan are not augmented by more specific and immediate objectives, it becomes difficult to measure progress in realizing goals. An annual updating of the plan, or an annual review of a standing plan, provides management with an opportunity to evaluate progress.

Periodic review of plans can be supplemented by other control procedures. The application of such mechanisms is especially desirable where a central systems staff is seeking to monitor progress by line operating divisions in implementing organization-wide goals.

STANDARDS

The issuance of standards for systems activities is a desirable end in itself. Standards can also help reinforce planning goals and establish technical constraints that are consistent with the systems plan. A comprehensive standards program should cover all aspects of systems development and operations, including acquisition and utilization of equipment and software, data communications, data base administration and application design and development.

Where planning goals encompass sharing not just equipment but also information resources, i.e., common elements of information, there should be standards to assure equipment and software compatability. This goes beyond specifying compatible equipment to standardizing programming languages and software packages for data base management.

A standards program should provide for the granting of exceptions when justified in particular situations. If, for example, the organization decides to use COBOL as the standard programming language, there may be circumstances in which assembly language is more suitable for a specialized application or in which the BASIC language is demonstrably more efficient for a particular minicomputer.

Flexibility in administering a standards program can be enhanced through the provision of options. For example, remote terminals could be classified into categories such as remote batch, intelligent and nonintelligent with specifications drawn up for each. Users could then acquire and operate terminals in any or all categories that met the standard terminal specifications. Similarly, a choice might be offered between a sophisticated high performance data base management software package requiring considerable training in its usage and a simple query package that is less efficient but easier to use.

Where standardization can be achieved in software, such as through high level programming languages and packages for data base management, the need for equipment standardization is less compelling. Programs written in a high level language can be readily converted from one type of equipment to another without the compatibility problems that have plagued computer users in the past. Indeed, where there is a heterogeneous mix of applications, it may be better *not* to standardize on equipment. Data processing applications can be most efficiently programmed in COBOL to run on a byte-oriented computer while scientific and engineering applications can more suitably be handled in FORTRAN and executed on a word-oriented computer. If there is a hierarchy of computers, it is likely that the features found most desirable in a locally operated minicomputer will not correspond to those found in a large central computer.

Communications technology is evolving increasingly in the direction of permitting the linking of multiple computers of different kinds, both large and small, into a common data network with relatively few compatibility constraints if all devices on the network adhere to standard communications protocols.

Application development standards can facilitate central staff review of projects undertaken in furtherance of planning goals and objectives. The adoption of a life cycle management approach, with standardized definitions of project phases and documentation of the end products of each phase, can provide agreed upon break points for monitoring progress. Adoption of a standardized project control method, such as the program evaluation and review technique (PERT) for major projects, can also aid in project review.

It is not our purpose here to outline all the features of a standards program. What should be stressed, though, is that control over the realization of systems planning objectives can be strengthened by carefully thought out standards. Standards can also ease the transition from one set of planning objectives to another when contingencies arise that necessitate a change in plans.

BUDGETS

Tying information systems planning into budget development and reporting provides a built-in set of controls for measuring performance against plan. In some organizations, the current and forthcoming budget year constitute the initial portion of the strategic plan and contain a great deal of specificity regarding objectives. When this is the case, each objective can be associated with a budgetary allocation to projects and activities supporting that objective.

Because budgets are usually developed according to object class, such as salaries, equipment rentals and supplies, it may be necessary to have a project cost accounting system in which charges are accumulated by project as well as by object class. Project budgets should then "cross foot" to the total object class budget, taking into account overhead activities not chargeable to a particular project. In this way, performance against plan can be measured for projects that are associated with planning objectives.

Where planning and budgeting are linked together, there is typically an annual cycle calling for review of planning objectives. Objectives are then modified based on the past year's operating experience and budget performance.

Cost studies in both industry and government show that personnel expenses constitute an increasingly large component of overall systems costs, in many cases exceeding fifty percent of total costs and overshadowing such other major cost elements as equipment purchases and rentals. Most of these personnel costs are attributable to application development and maintenance rather than computer operations. With the advent of operating systems software, remote data entry and other sophisticated techniques, machine room operations are becoming less labor intensive.

The increase in personnel costs for application development is due to several factors. One is the improvement in price-performance capabilities of computing equipment as a result of advances in both equipment and software technology. Another is the increasing burden of maintaining a growing portfolio of user applications while at the same time responding to demands for new application projects.

Regardless of the reasons for rising personnel costs, they merit special attention in efforts to control performance in implementing planning objectives. Because most objectives require application development, a highly labor intensive activity, the efficient use of personnel resources should receive special scrutiny. Techniques to improve the productivity of analysts and programmers, such as the methodology of "structured" application design and programming, along with a strong standards program, should be considered to improve the budgetary performance of computer projects and minimize cost overruns.

PROCUREMENTS

Central staff approval of the acquisition of data processing equipment provides an effective way to control divisional plans that call for additional capacity. Procurement control can be applied to decentralized divisions that operate their own computer facilities; it can also be a tool for top management control over central staff computer facility operations.

Control over procurement is especially meaningful in government agencies in which equipment is usually acquired through competitive bidding. This involves the preparation of detailed specifications to provide the basis for submission of vendor proposals. It frequently requires a protracted time schedule, anywhere from ninety days to over a year for a large-scale system, to prepare the specifications, seek bids, evaluate proposals, conduct benchmarks and perform acceptance testing. Central staff review of proposed acquisitions should take place early in this procurement cycle to provide more opportunity for influencing the strategies that underlie the request for new equipment.

In the private sector, especially in smaller firms, procurement procedures and practices are not so rigorous, and competitive bidding is not always the practice. There is, however, usually a requirement for top management approval of large capital investments. Because data processing equipment often represents a sizable investment, there is opportunity for the central staff review of such capital expenditure requests as an adjunct to the customary top management review.

Though control over procurement offers a ready opportunity for the planning staff to review -- and challenge -- systems plans throughout the organization that call for new equipment, the deficiencies of this control mechanism must be recognized. First, it is incomplete. Not every new application initiated by a user requires additional equipment capability; it may be made operational on existing equipment already under control of the user. Where data processing services are provided centrally to users, new applications requirements become intermingled with other demands for increased capacity at the central facility, such as normal increases in transaction processing volumes. If a user is but one of dozens or hundreds served by a central facility, it is difficult to associate the need for expansion of equipment capacity with the applications plans of any one user.

To prevent procurement control from becoming unwieldy, a lower limit must be placed on central staff review of equipment acquisitions. In the federal government, for example, the General Services Administration must approve the procurement of equipment or software with a purchase price of more than $500,000. Though such a threshold will cause scrutiny of large acquisitions, significant systems capacity can today be acquired within this dollar limitation. In fact, a user could develop a large network of interconnected minicomputers, acquired one by one as the need for capacity increased, with each purchase falling below the approval threshold. In companies in which there must be approval for capital investments, central controls can be bypassed merely by leasing the equipment.

But the chief weakness in procurement control as a means of enforcing adherence to planning objectives lies not in the loopholes that can be found in any approval procedure, but in the stage in the project life cycle at which new equipment requirements are identified. Even in government agencies, in which the procurement process is more visible and more protracted, considerable planning activity necessarily precedes the documentation of new requirements specifications included in a request for proposals. Where plans have been formulated and given the approval of divisional management, and are accompanied by justification in the form of feasibility studies and cost-benefit analyses, it will be difficult to disapprove or redirect a project effort by the time the request for procurement approval is received. Too often, those responsible for reviewing procurement actions are confronted with a "fait accompli" and have little choice but to accede to the request.

PRIOR APPROVALS

1. Project plans. Project planning has already been discussed as it relates to strategic systems planning. A formalized method of justifying and initiating application development projects and reviewing progress toward completion provides a means of controlling adherence to planning strategies. Central staff review of significant project plans during the initiation phase can help determine that application projects are being undertaken in furtherance of planning goals and that resources are not being diverted to low priority projects.

   In establishing project review procedures, as in the case of equipment acquisition approvals, a reasonable threshold should be established to permit user autonomy and to avoid inundating the planning staff with reviews of trivial project proposals.

   Though projects may be identified in budget formulation, prior approval of project plans is essentially independent of the budgetary review cycle. Projects may be initiated at any time and their duration may span several budgetary periods. If the life cycle management concept is well established, major projects can be monitored at various milestones in their life cycle.

2. Organizational changes. A requirement for central staff review of proposed changes in divisional systems units offers a good opportunity for control. Does the reorganization further the division's ability to implement planning objectives or does it possibly contravene these targets? Will additional resources be required to support an expanded organization that might better be allocated to high priority projects elsewhere in the business?

    If organization planning procedures call for drafting of functional statements, these can be reviewed to make sure that the responsibility for systems planning within each division is specifically set forth. And if a staffing plan is also required, this can be examined to determine whether adequate staff resources are being allocated to strategic planning.

3. Personnel actions. Another form of prior approval that can strengthen control over implementation of plans is review of personnel actions affecting systems professionals. If line divisions have their own systems people, there may be merit in requiring central staff approval of new hires, promotions and reassignments. In this way, staff increases can be controlled and assurance gained that personnel are being assigned to activities sanctioned in the systems plan.

    As in the case of project and organizational plans, review of personnel actions is independent of the budgetary process. The availability of funds in divisional budgets for additional systems people does not mean necessarily that such personnel should be brought on board unless their contributions are directed toward objectives that have a high priority from an organization-wide planning standpoint.

    To avoid undue interference in divisional personnel management, thresholds can be established in terms of salary levels or position grade levels so that only the more senior professional slots require prior approval. There is little to be gained in subjecting computer operators and those asigned to repetitive tasks like data entry to prior approval.

As is true of any control mechanism, good faith is necessary on the part of line management in obtaining prior approval of either project plans, reorganizations or personnel assignments. Projects can, for example, be divided into subtasks to stay under prior approval thresholds. And personnel actions can be disguised by diverting non-computer people to the performance of data processing tasks. To the extent that there is a lack of harmony and rapport throughout the organization in supporting planning goals, there will always be ample opportunity for line management to thwart organization-wide strategy and to emphasize divisional interests at the expense of broader objectives.

4.3 SCOPE AND FORMAT OF PLANS

It is difficult to generalize regarding the exact scope and content of an "ideal" strategic planning document. Plans vary markedly from one organization to another in their coverage and level of detail.

Figure 4-1 provides an outline of the contents of the strategic plan of one large organization. (2)

A Large business firm classifies planning into two categories: those pertaining to information systems design and those pertaining to information systems management. Within each category there are several goals organized according to sub-categories, as for example in information systems design:

1.   Applications to support functional management
2.   Unified organization-wide applications
3.   Data management
4.   Standards development

Each of thes planning subcategories contains a brief statement of a planning goal, usually a single sentence. This is followed by a summary of the strategy needed to

The following chapter outline has been adopted from the actual strategic plan of a large organization to illustrate items that should be covered in the preparation of a typical plan.

Chapter 1. The Planning Process: This chapter contains sections summarizing general concepts of information systems planning; a description of the planning cycle for the organization, i.e., deadlines for submission of divisional planning documents to corporate headquarters; and a general description of the procedures to be followed in performing systems planning. Like all chapters in the plan, the discussion is presented in nontechnical terms that a line manager could understand.

Chapter 2. Historical Development: The sections of this chapter describe the history of computer usage in the company. Early experience is summarized in one section describing events up to 1970; a second section covers 1970 through 1975; and a final section discusses events since 1975. The format of this chapter is such that additional summary material can be added without requiring a complete revision.

Chapter 3. Strategic Planning Goals: This is the heart of the strategic plan. It contains a description of the technological environment which the planners expect to prevail over the next five years, followed by goals statements and and discussion of each goal. The chapter is organized into the following sections:

A. Information Management
B. Computer Facility Management
C. Management Science Methods
D. Application Development
E. Data Communications
F. Security and Privacy Protection
G. Organization and Personnel

Chapter 4. Resource Utilization: This chapter contains a variety of exhibits presenting quantitative data about trends in data processing within the company based on historical data. Included are such items as growth in numbers of terminals; investment in equipment; hardware inventory in terms of large CPU's, terminals and minicomputers; tabulations of average cost per job for each major computer center; and distribution of dollar resources among personnel, equipment, data communications and outside services. Augmenting this historical trend data are five-year projections of expenditures and other indicators of systems growth.

Chapter 5. Divisional Plans: This chapter includes one section for each of the twenty autonomous divisions of the company. Each section contains an organization chart; a planning narative; an inventory of equipment installed, on order and planned; and five-year projections of numbers of employees in each systems group and the estimated budget of each group.

Figure 4-1/Outline of Systems Plan

realize the goal. The strategy statement is set forth in a brief paragraph. For instance, the data management category includes the following:

Goal: To develop a system that will improve the control, availability and integrity of the data required to support all levels of management and operations.

Strategy: Develop a single dictionary/directory of data commonly required by the operating divisions. Develop uniform data management practices and standards for interdivisional data. (3)

Figures 4-2 through 4-6 present the tables of contents of several plans from both public and private sector organizations. These plans range in length from a scant dozen or so pages to multiple volumes of detailed baseline information and projections. Though one expert has asserted that "when you see a three-inch thick planning binder sitting on the shelf, you're probably looking at $50,000 to $100,000 worth of wasted effort," in actuality there are short plans that suffer from superficiality and lengthy plans that provide an excellent road map for the systems organization. (4) One factor that affects the scope of the strategic plan is the extent to which project plans are included as backup material to support goals and objectives. Another has to do with whether detailed budgetary data covering the first year or two of the plan is included.

Considering these and other plans as indicative of content coverage, a thoroughly articulated plan should, in some form and sequence, contain:

1. Executive Summary

2. Profile of Existing Capability

    - Equipment
    - Software
    - Personnel

3. Usage Projections

MAJOR OIL COMPANY
TEN YEAR PLAN

1.   Introduction

2.   Management Summary

3.   Systems Environment

4.   Application Systems Plan

5.   Resource Plan

6.   Resource Forecast

7.   Communications Plan

8.   Technology Forecast

9.   Goals/Objectives/Actions

10. Planning Cycle

Figure 4-2

MILITARY AGENCY
MASTER PLAN

1. Executive Summary

2. Introduction

3. Threat, Information Needs and Policy

4. Goals and Objectives

5. Long Term System Architecture

6. System Baseline

7. Implementation

8. Glossary

Figure 4-3

FEDERAL AGENCY
TEN YEAR PLAN

1. Executive Summary

2. Introduction

3. Data Automation Background

4. Technology Opportunities

5. Conclusions

6. Recommendations and Timetable

Figure 4-4

STATE GOVERNMENT
THREE YEAR PLAN

1. Introduction

2. Mission

   A. Organization

   B. Financing

   C. User Community

   D. Advisory Groups

   E. Computer Resources

3. Accomplishments

4. Data Processing Plan

   A. Assumptions

   B. Goals

   C. Strategies

   D. Objectives

Figure 4-5

FINANCE COMPANY
THREE YEAR PLAN

---

1. Overview

2. Position Statement: Centralized vs. Decentralized

3. Action Replacement Strategy

4. Systems Development

5. Hardware

6. Communications

7. Operations and Technical Support

8. Planning and Coordination

9. Human Resources

10. User Support

Figure 4-6

4. Planning Goals and Objectives -- grouped into logical categories

5. Strategies -- including delineation of alternative plans

6. Assumptions on

    -   Policy
    -   Technology
    -   Environment

7. Constraints

To this might be added supplementary sections that further delineate goals, objectives and strategies, along with project plans that provide resource estimates and schedules for achieving planned objectives. (4)

Just as there is a wide variety in the coverage of individual strategic plans, there is similar diversity in the instructions issued to guide the preparation of such plans. Sometimes the instructions are more exhaustive than the resultant planning document, containing detailed procedures, examples and forms for the collection of planning data.

4.4 GUIDELINES FOR PLANNING

Because the need for systems planning is only now beginning to receive the recognition it deserves, it is not surprising that one can find few generally accepted principles for performing such planning. The following are offered as guidelines in the hope that they may stimulate thinking and concern about the planning process:

1. Make provision in the systems plan for taking small steps rapidly. This will help to avoid the pitfall of "ultimate" systems goals that have no immediate objectives or operational subphases. It may indeed be desirable to look ahead to the millenium of an "integrated, total" management information system. But the attainment of such an ultimate goal should be a step-by-step process which permits the organization to receive the economic bene-

fits of applications that can be made operational in the immediate future but are consistent with longer range systems goals.

2. Develop alternative plans when significant contradictory trends are discerned in the business or technological environment. As we have mentioned, consideration of alternatives becomes almost mandatory in planning beyond a five-year period. Technology assessment can play a significant role in structuring alternative systems plans.

3. Interface the systems plan with the corporate plan, modifying both appropriately. If there is no explicitly stated corporate plan, as is still frequently the case today, the systems planner must then make planning assumptions about the nature of corporate goals. These should be made part of the systems plan.

4. Document the systems plan in a format intelligible to top management, and arrange for a personal presentation. One of the voids in the relationship between systems people and executive management is that management is typically approached only to gain approval for the acquisition of a particular piece of equipment or to obtain the go-ahead for a certain application project. The systems plan, documented in nontechnical jargon and presented to policy level management, can give the "big picture" of the systems function and aid in gaining an appreciation of its importance.

5. Establish a formal mechanism for review and reiteration of the systems plan. Because there must be feedback and interaction among the various contributors to the plan, the planning process is a continuing one. With the rapidity of change so evident in the field of computer technology, modifications will be required, not only because of experience gained within the organization but because of forces at work outside.

6. Develop methods for maintaining an inventory of equipment and software and for measuring and projecting utilization of installed equipment. This is necessary so that the useful life of equipment -- and software -- can be considered in the systems plan.

7. Fix the organizational responsibility for systems planning. In large organizations there should be a director of systems planning; in smaller organizations, the responsibility should be assigned to a designated individual, even though this may be only a part-time duty.

8. Rotate the assignment of personnel to the planning staff. This enables key people throughout the organization to gain new perspectives by exposure to the strategic planning process.

9. Budget for technology assessment. This is important in order to permit first-hand evaluation of new equipment and systems techniques without the pressure of cost justification that is usually associated with approval of new projects or the acquisition of new equipment.

10. Set up a comparative systems intelligence activity. Because systems planning does have importance as a competitive weapon, it is desirable to determine the existing capability and the future plans of competitors. This does not require "industrial espionage" as much as a painstaking review of the public pronouncements of these competitors and their equipment suppliers plus reliance on the time-honored weapon of industry contacts.

There are no doubt other points that could be cited as contributory to the development and maintenance of a soundly conceived strategic systems plan. The most important considerations are, however, that the significance of systems planning be understood by management and that the development of a plan, however primitive, be undertaken.

NOTES

1. Within IBM, "the information systems control and planning organization, which also included an (information systems) architecture function, grew to 16 in 1967, 33 in 1968, and peaked at 36 in 1969. In 1974 20 people were concerned with information systems control and planning." P. Duane Walker in Ephraim R. McLean and John V. Snoden, "Strategic Planning for MIS," New York, John Wiley and Son, Inc., 1977, p. 176.

2. Adapted from the a strategic plan prepared under the direction of the author.

3. Adapted from an outline of the IBM systems plan as presented by Walker in McLean and Soden, pp. 172-174. This text also includes descriptions of plans produced by other organizations, most notably TRW, p. 132, and Los Angeles Unified School District, pp. 313-314.

4. For a discussion of the pros and cons of systems planning documentation by several MIS directors and consultants, see Martin Lasden, "Long-range Planning: Curse or Blessing?" Computer Decisions, February, 1981, pp. 103-109.

5. A slightly lengthier set of guidelines, with a somewhat different emphasis, is offered by John V. Snowden and Charles C. Tucker in "Long Range MIS Planning," Journal of Systems Management, July 1976, pp. 28-33.

Appendix
Assessing Systems Planning Effectiveness

This Appendix was adapted, with substantial modification, from a report by the Financial and General Management Studies Division of the U.S. General Accounting Office. The need for an evaluation guide was recognized by the GAO staff as a result of over 42 reviews during the past 15 years where the management of U.S. agency information systems planning was found to be inadequate.

In the review guide, the information systems (IS) planning process is divided into five major subject areas, and a section is devoted to each. They are:

1. Organization

2. Direction

3. Structure

4. Control

5. Reporting

In each section the essential elements for that subject are identified by a two-digit number, e.g.;

1.3 Establish an Executive Management Committee

Each essential element (two-digit number) is then amplified by a series of questions identified by three and four-digit numbers, e.g.,

1.3.1 Has an executive management (or steering) committee been established?

1.3.1.1 Is there a formal charter issued by the chief executive?

Note that in some instances questions have been repeated in more than one section in the interests of including a complete set of elements for each section. In many places, the original GAO terminology has been changed to reflect the business planning environment. Suggested symbols for recording answers to the questions are provided below:

Symbol	Meaning of Symbol
S	The task is being performed (or the action indicated is being taken) in a satisfactory manner.
U	The task is being performed (or the action indicated is being taken) but the result appears unsatisfactory.
NP	The task (or action) is considered necessary but is not being performed.
NA	The task (or action) is considered not applicable for the particular criteria.

With few exceptions, the greater the number of "U" or "NP" answers, the more serious are the management problems.

GAO cautions that these criteria represent idealized performance objectives. For example, no organization will meet all the criteria exactly as presented. In many cases, substitute procedures, abbreviated measures or other approaches would be as effective as those identified here. An ability to recognize such substitutions and sufficient understanding of planning principles to make confident judgments about their effectiveness are essential for anyone using this appendix.

CONTENTS

1. ORGANIZATION

    1.1   Establish Responsibility and Accountability for IS Plans

    1.2   Hold Functional Managers Responsible for Strategy in IS Plans

    1.3   Establish a Systems Steering Committee

    1.4   Establish a Central Planning Staff

    1.5   Provide Directives for Integration of Systems

    1.6   Assess the Tradeoffs between Risks and Potential Payoff

    1.7   Develop a Financial Forecast

    1.8   Review the Financial Forecast

    1.9   Require Accountability for IS Investments

    1.10   Establish Top Management Decision Points

2. DIRECTION

    2.1   Identify Company Goals

    2.2   Identify Long-Range Company Plans

    2.3   Translate Company Objectives into IS Goals

    2.4   Identify the Strategy for Achieving IS Goals

2.5   Establish the Scope of Centralized Authority

2.6   Require Accountability for Approval of IS Requirements

2.7   Assign Priorities for IS Requirements

2.8   Consolidate Long-Range Plans

2.9   Identify IS Investment Risks

2.10   Require Supporting Strategies

2.11   Assign Responsibility for Carrying Out the Plan

3. STRUCTURE

3.1   Identify the Organizational Structure for IS Planning

3.2   Require Life Cycle Projections for Software Applications

3.3   Require Life Cycle Projections for the Hardware Configuration

3.4   Standardize the Life Cycle Planning Structure

3.5   Test the Translation from Functional to Technical Specifications

3.6   Require Compliance with Standards

3.7   Establish a Planning Time Frame

3.8   Maintain Planning Policies and Procedures Up-to-date

3.9   Require a List of Long-Range Objectives

3.10   Include Planning Assumptions

3.11   Amplify the IS Objectives

3.12   Expose Support Problems

3.13   Exploit New Opportunities

3.14   Identify the Potential for External Support

3.15   Perform an Economic Analysis

3.16   Require a Risk Assessment

3.17   Provide for Plan Implementation

4.   CONTROL

4.1   State All Performance Criteria

4.2   Require that Performance Criteria Be Quantified

4.3   Quantify User Requirements

4.4   Quantify Expected Benefits

4.5   Quantify Existing Software Assets

4.6   Require that Proposed New or Revised Applications Be Quantified

4.7   Quantify Existing Hardware Capability

4.8   Require that Proposed Hardware Acquisitions Be Quantified

4.9   Quantify Existing System Products

4.10   Require that Proposed Outputs Be Quantified

4.11   Require that Development Risk Be Quantified

5.   REPORTING

5.1   Require Organization-wide Resource Accounting and Control

5.2   Provide Life Cycle Costing

5.3   Require Reports on Implementation of the IS Plan

5.4   Require a Software Inventory Report

5.5   Require a Hardware Inventory Report

5.6   Require Auditor Review and Report on Plans

1. ORGANIZATION

Some degree of active involvement in plan formulation is essential for all levels of an organization that might be affected when the plans are carried out. For Information Systems (IS) planning it is critical that this active involvement be formalized and made visible at three key organizational levels: top management, IS management, and user management.

Evidence of formalized involvement at each of these levels should be conspicuous and well communicated within the organization. The form of that evidence and its substance are both important. In this section the essential elements of involvement by top management, IS management and user management are identified.

1.1   Establish Responsibility and Accountability for IS Plans

Through written policies and guidelines the chief executive should establish responsibilities and accountability for IS planning.

1.1.1   Are senior managers of each major organizational unit required to
o   participate in the planning?
o   define their long-range IS requirements?

1.2   Hold Functional Managers Responsible for Strategy in IS Plans

Require that the head of each major organizational unit be responsible and held accountable for the decisions affecting his unit which are included in the strategy for achieving the IS objectives.

1.2.1   Do senior managers of each major organizational unit require that those subordinate managers who use DP output participate in long-range IS planning?

1.2.2   Are subordinate managers held accountable for the determination, justification and long-range planning of their IS requirements?

1.2.2.1   Are subordinate managers required to confirm the value of the existing DP support they receive in terms of its contribution to performance of their functional tasks?

1.2.2.2   Are systems cost allocated to each user?

1.2.2.3   Are subordinate managers instructed to justify their long-range IS requirements in terms of payoff contributions made to the functions for which they are responsible?

1.2.2.4   Are subordinate managers instructed to show the gap between existing procedures and required IS support?

1.2.2.5   Are subordinate managers required to use quantitative terms to identify the performance criteria which, when achieved, will close the gap?

1.2.2.6   Was an estimated cost considered by these subordinate managers when they inserted their requirements into the long-range plan?

1.2.2.7   Was this estimated cost based on a life cycle projection for the system that would satisfy the requirements?

1.2.2.8   Are subordinate managers held accountable when computer systems developed for their support fall short of expected performance?

1.2.2.9   Are subordinate managers required to evaluate and take a position on cost benefit forecasts of systems being developed for their support?

1.3   Establish a Systems Steering Committee

A formal executive management (or systems steering) committee consisting of senior management from major organizational units should be established. Subject only to review by the chief executive, it should be held responsible for consolidation and integration of both the functional and the technical aspects of information systems.

1.3.1   Has an executive management (or steering) committee been established? (We will use the term steering committee.)

1.3.1.1   Is there a formal charter issued by the chief executive which describes the responsibilities, authority and duties of the steering committee?

1.3.1.2   Does the charter require the chairman of the steering committee to report results of the committee's work directly to the chief executive?

1.3.1.3   Does the charter require that steering committee disagreements be presented to the chief executive for a decision?

1.3.2   Does the charter also establish a working group for the steering committee whose duties are to research the issues, perform intraorganizational coordination and other preparatory work supportive to the steering committee?

1.3.2.1   Does each member of the steering committee have a representative on the steering committee working group?

1.3.3   Is the steering committee required to review, approve or indicate disagreement with the long-range IS plan produced by the central planning staff?

1.4   Establish a Central Planning Staff

This staff should be established within the information systems function to prepare the company-wide IS plan and coordinate the IS planning activities of all other organizational units.

1.4.1   Has the authority and responsibility of a central planning staff been established by a written charter?

1.4.2   Where there is no central planning staff is there a planning or coordinating group with similar responsibilities?

1.4.3   Do the written duties and responsibilities of the members of the central planning staff require them to produce planning products for which they can be held accountable?

1.5   Provide Directives for Integration of Systems

The central planning staff should be held responsible and accountable for integration of systems across departmental lines of authority.

1.5.1   Do the written duties of the central planning staff require that it produce a company-wide integrated long-range plan for approval by the chief executive or the steering committee?

1.5.2   Is the central planning staff required to review all systems plans and assess the potential for integration of systems across the entire company?

1.5.2.1   Does the central planning staff analyze and assess for overlap and integration potential each organizational unit's

- o   support applications?
- o   IS objectives and sub-objectives?
- o   expected performance criteria?
- o   support problems?
- o   proposed new opportunities?
- o   potential for systems integration?

1.5.3   Is the central planning staff required to document the results of its assessments?

> 1.5.3.1   Does the head of each major functional unit coordinate the systems recommendations made by the central planning staff?

1.5.4   Do the results of the central planning staff studies substantially influence the system design concepts and the technical design of IS applications?

1.6   Assess the Tradeoffs Between Risks and Potential Payoff

The central planning staff should be held responsible for identifying and assessing the organization-wide risks and the value of the potential payoff of the total IS investment.

1.6.1   For each objective in the IS plan, is there an accompanying statement of the performance criteria expected when the objectives or sub-objectives are achieved?

1.6.2   Does the central planning staff determine whether the objectives in all IS plans contain sufficient quantitative performance criteria to be used in a cost benefit analysis?

1.6.3   Where such performance criteria are not included with the objectives, is there some other basis in the planning documentation which communicates how achievement of the objectives will be recognized?

1.6.4   Are the performance criteria which describe how the achievement of objectives will be recognized presented in quantitative terms?

1.6.5   Can the gap between existing and planned capabilities be identified from the record?

        1.6.5.1   Has the central planning staff focused on those gaps as a means of identifying what the planned investment in IS resources will buy?

        1.6.5.2   Has the central planning staff reviewed the impact of this gap in IS capabilities and reported in writing its assessment and recommendations?

1.6.6   Is the central planning staff required to identify to top management those applications which

    o   have high technical risks?
    o   have high operational risks?

1.6.7   Is the central planning staff required to establish a quantitative mission "payoff" ranking for each application contained in the long-range plan?

1.6.8   Is the manager of each major unit required to coordinate, or dissent with, the mission payoff assessment identified by the central planning staff?

1.7   Develop a Financial Forecast

The central planning staff should develop a company-wide coordinated financial forecast of the overall costs of all IS resources for each year over the life of the long-range plan.

1.7.1   Has each major unit manager been required to include in his long-range IS plan a list of those applications which he uses but which provide unsatisfactory support or which have only a marginal payoff to the efficiency, effectiveness and economy of operations?

        1.7.1.1   Are the unsatisfactory or marginal support capabilities identified in quantitative terms?

1.7.2   Is each functional manager required to list in his long-range IS plans those IS applications which provide satisfactory support?

1.7.3   Is each functional manager required to identify those existing applications whose modification or enhancement would increase the efficiency, economy and effectiveness of operations?

        1.7.3.1   Is there a requirement to describe these modifications or enhancements in quantitative terms?

1.7.4   Is there a requirement that functional managers identify new IS capabilities that will increase the effectiveness of their operations?

        1.7.4.1   Are these new requirements for support identified in quantitative terms?

1.7.5   Has the head of each organizational unit prepared a list of applications available from an external source that would result in increased productivity or some other "payoff" if acquired?

1.7.5.1   For each proposed external support application, is the estimated cost included?

1.8   Review the Financial Forecast

Top management should review the financial forecast and formalize, in writing, investment decisions and priorities.

1.8.1   For each year of the plan, does the financial forecast show the costs attributable to each major organizational unit?

1.8.2   For each year of the plan, does the financial forecast show the costs of the IS operation by major systems components such as

o   hardware?
o   systems software?
o   application software?
o   peripherals?
o   communications?
o   other components?

1.8.3   Are the costs shown in a consistent format from year to year?

1.8.4   Are cost trends shown?

1.8.5   Is the priority shown for each application along with its annual and total cumulative life cycle cost estimate?

1.9   Require Accountability for IS Investments

The senior manager of each organizational unit that receives or provides support should be formally assigned, in writing, the responsibility and accountability for investment decisions made as a result of his stated support requirements and recommendations.

    1.9.1   Does the record show that the senior manager reviewed and approved

        o   the financial forecast contained in the long-range plan?

        o   the priority of resource investments contained in the long-range plan?

1.10   Establish Top Management Decision Points

Key phases (or milestones), such as those in the life cycle of each major software application, should be established in the plan as decision points where the chief executive personally makes the decision to continue to the next phase.

    1.10.1   Does the chief executive have a regularly scheduled review of the "expected" performance against "actual" performance contained in the IS plan?

    1.10.2   Are shortfalls between planned performance and actual performance identified on a systematic basis?

    1.10.3   Is there a standard set of decision points by which the actual performance against planned performance is followed? (This can be milestones such as those in the life cycle of a software application.)

2. DIRECTION

Specific direction and guidance must be provided throughout the systems planning process to achieve consistent and effective plans. This direction is obtained from the organization's mission requirements. Based on these requirements, goals and objectives are established, and a coordinated strategy for achieving them is developed and included in the plan. Policies and procedures are formalized in writing to assure that the strategy is communicated to those who carry out the plan.

2.1   Identify Company Goals

IS plans should identify the missions or goals contained in policy documents.

2.1.1   Are company missions or goals available in a written document?

2.2   Identify Long-Range Plans

Long-range plans which provide the basis for IS support requirements should be identified and described. (NOTE: These are not the IS plans but they provide the basis for IS plans.)

2.2.1   Is there documentation which describes the strategies to achieve company goals?

2.2.1.1   Does this documentation contain the short- and long-range objectives to be achieved for each goal?

2.2.1.2   Is there sufficient quantitative or other explicit information contained in the statement of objectives to provide effective criteria for assessing when objectives are actually achieved?

2.2.2   Is there documentation that shows that the head of each organizational unit does assess trends for impact on his unit's functional tasks, i.e.,

o   political trends?
o   technical trends?
o   social trends?
o   work trends?

2.2.2.1   Based on the type of assessment, are factors or assumptions developed which influence the content of long-range IS plans?

2.2.3   Are assumptions included as an integral part of the long-range IS plan?

2.2.3.1   Is there any evidence that the chief executive reviewed the IS planning assumptions and approved them?

2.3   Translate Company Objectives into IS Goals

Company objectives should be translated into IS goals which support achievement of objectives, and these should be documented.

2.3.1   Is there documentation which shows the IS goals that support achievement of company objectives?

2.4   Identify the Strategy for Achieving IS Goals

The plan should contain a strategy or series of decisions which indicate how IS goals are to be achieved.

2.4.1   Is there documentation for a strategy to accomplish each IS goal, i.e., a set of decisions which have been made?

2.4.1.1   Does this strategy contain long-range objectives?

2.4.1.2   Are these long-range objectives stated quantitatively?

2.4.1.3   Do the long-range objectives provide a guide for the investment of IS resources?

2.4.1.4   Does the strategy contain quantitatively stated short-range objectives?

2.5   Establish the Scope of Centralized Authority

There should be clear policy expression of the authority, responsibility and accountability for information systems resources. This should cover control of planning, design, development and operations, and compliance with policies and standards. It should specifically establish the degree to which such control is or is not centralized at company headquarters.

2.5.1   Is there policy documentation concerning

2.5.1.1   Internal organizational authority to spend IS funds?

2.5.1.2   responsibility for IS resource use?

2.5.1.3   accountability for IS resource investment results?

2.5.2   Is there documentation which assigns responsibility and accountability for

2.5.2.1   planning the use of IS resources?

2.5.2.2   design of systems?

2.5.2.3   development of systems?

2.5.2.4   operational performance of systems?

2.5.2.5   compliance with policies and standards?

2.5.3   Does this documentation establish the degree to which control is centralized at company headquarters?

2.6   Require Accountability for Approval of IS Requirements

Accountability for cost effective IS applications lies with the senior manager who approved the requirement for that support. This should be established as a matter of written policy.

2.6.1   Is there documentation which assigns authority for approval of IS requirements?

2.6.2   Does this documentation require that estimated cost figures accompany the IS requirements request or otherwise be known before the requirement is approved?

2.6.3   Are there provisions to hold the approving official(s) accountable for the payoff of resource investment? (I.e., are there start, finish and use milestones or checkpoints where the signature or initials of the approving official(s) are required as acknowledgement of control, feedback, status and payoff?)

2.7   Assign Priorities for IS Requirements

There should be an established procedure to assign priorities for IS requirements. This procedure should be consistent with top management's investment priorities.

2.7.1   Is there a documented procedure which requires establishment of priorities for the investment of IS resources?

2.7.2   Is the actual setting of investment priorities consistent with the procedures set by top management?

2.8   Consolidate Long-Range Plans

The central IS planning staff should consolidate long-range IS plans developed by the functional units and prepare a company-wide systems plan. This staff should determine whether the subordinate plans contain sufficient quantitative measures for use in cost benefit analyses.

2.8.1   Is there a written directive establishing the central IS planning staff?

2.8.2   Is the central planning staff tasked to consolidate all long-range IS plans developed by functional managers and prepare a company-wide systems plan?

2.8.3   Has the central planning staff been assigned to determine whether the IS objectives proposed in functional unit plans are consistent with company objectives?

2.8.4   Has the central planning staff been assigned to determine whether the objectives in functional unit's IS plans contain sufficient quantitative performance criteria to be used in a cost benefit analysis?

2.8.5   Has the central planning staff been assigned to report to top management its findings on each item listed above?

2.9   Identify IS Investment Risks

The central planning staff should document IS investment risks which require top management attention. These can be identified by a lack of quantitative criteria and vague linkage between IS objectives and company objectives.

2.9.1   Is the central planning staff required to identify to top management those applications which

         o   have high technical risks?

o   have high operational risks?

2.9.2   Is the central planning staff required to establish a quantitative mission "payoff" ranking for each application contained in the plan?

2.9.3   Is the head of each major functional unit required to coordinate, or dissent with, the mission payoff assessment identified by the central planning staff?

2.10   Require Supporting Strategies

The head of each major organizational unit should summarize the key decisions that form the basis of the long-range IS plans for his unit. These decisions, or assumed decisions, should also be included in the long-range plan.

2.10.1   Is publication of an IS strategy required as part of, or associated with, the long-range systems plan?

2.10.2   Does the strategy consolidate the long-range objectives proposed by the heads of the different major functional units?

2.10.3   Does the strategy identify the performance gap which the investment in IS resources is intended to overcome?

2.10.4   Is there a quantitative expression of the payoff to mission performance that will be purchased by the resource investments in the long-range IS plan?

2.10.4.1   Is this payoff identified on an annual basis for each year covered by the long-range IS plan?

2.10.5   Is there a requirement for the IS strategy to contain an investment priority ranking for the applications listed in the long-range IS plan?

2.10.6   Is there a requirement for the manager of each major functional unit to coordinate the priority ranking submitted to the
central planning staff?

2.10.7   Is there a requirement for the chief executive to indicate his
written approval of the decisions contained in the strategy
document?

2.11   Assign Responsibility for Carrying Out the Plan

Responsibility and accountability for carrying out the plan should
normally be along the lines of organizational authority. When a steering committee or a project team is used, their authority and responsibility should be specified.

2.11.1   Is there a set of documents which indicate that the individual
responsible for carrying out the plan is aware of his responsibilities and authority?

2.11.2   Have organizational unit managers been informed concerning
the responsibility and authority of those carrying out the
plan?

2.11.3   Does the record show any confusion or lack of authoritative
direction in the carrying out of the plan?

2.11.4   Is there documentation which assigns responsibility and
accountability for maintaining the written planning regulations, instruction and guidelines up to date?

2.11.4.1   Is there a senior official who reports directly to
the chief executive assigned this responsibility?

2.11.4.2   If the answer is "no," is the organizational location of the responsible individual at an authoritative level above that of the major department
heads?

3. STRUCTURE

The primary purpose of the systems plan is to direct and control the investment of
IS resources. To accomplish this purpose, a structure of short- and long-range
plans must be developed. This structure should provide for the short-term operational needs of each organizational unit as well as their future requirements. A
company-wide IS plan should be the product of established planning procedures.

The elements of the IS planning structure should be formalized, documented and
communicated to all units of the organization that may be affected by the plan.
These elements may vary somewhat, but in all companies there is a minimum
structure essential to a sound IS planning capability. That minimum is described
in this section.

3.1   Identify the Organizational Structure for IS Planning

The structure and framework showing authority, responsibility and
accountability for systems planning in each organizational unit affected by, or participating in, the planning should be documented and
disseminated.

3.1.1   Can an organizational structure for IS planning be identified
from documentation issued at headquarters (policy) level?

3.1.2   Is documentation describing the organizational structure for
IS planning available at each level of management whose
subordinates use output from the information system?

3.1.3   Are non-management employees, whose job performance is
affected by IS output, aware of the organizational structure

for IS planning?

3.2   Require Life Cycle Projections for Software Applications

Planning should cover the entire period during which resources will be spent on each application.

3.2.1   Do the long-range planning instructions require, or the plan include, a set of time phased, standard decision points, or milestones, over the life cycle of each application?

3.2.2   Do the long-range planning instructions require, or the plan include, a management evaluation of the technical and economic effectiveness of an application as part of each milestone?

3.2.3   Do planning instructions require, or does the plan include, an information base (feasibility study or other analysis) which supports, for each application, the requirements and management's decision for

o   continuation of the application?
o   development of the application?
o   conversion of the application?
o   redesign of the application?
o   termination of the application?

3.2.3.1   Are milestones, similar to the following, included in the life cycle projection for each application?

(a)   requirements analysis?
(b)   development?
(c)   production?
(d)   redesign (or termination)?
(e)   conversion (or termination)?

3.2.4   The operational efficiency of the computer system is an essential component of the planning base. One method for identifying its level of operational efficiency is through the computation and use of efficiency ratios. (The computation method for these ratios will vary for different types of systems -- such as one that can be multi-programmed.)

3.2.4.1   Is the efficiency of the existing computer operation expressed in the plan by means of performance ratios or some equivalent method?

3.2.4.2   Is there an application production run ratio? (This ratio is obtained when the number of production runs is divided by the total number of all runs for a specified period. For example, a weekly production run ratio might be the number of production runs divided by the total number of all runs for that week.)

$$\frac{\text{Production runs}}{\text{Total of all runs}} = \text{Production run ratio}$$

3.2.4.3   Is there an application maintenance run ratio? (This ratio is obtained by dividing the maintenance runs by the total number of all runs for a specified period.)

$$\frac{\text{Application maintenance runs}}{\text{Total of all runs}} = \text{Application maintenance run ratio}$$

3.2.4.4   Is there an application development run ratio? (This ratio is obtained by dividing the total development runs by the total number of all runs for the period specified.)

$$\frac{\text{Total number of development runs}}{\text{Total of all runs}} = \begin{array}{l}\text{Application}\\ \text{development}\\ \text{run ratio}\end{array}$$

3.2.4.5   Over the past three years, is there any indication that ratios similar to those above were used to inform management as to trends in

- o   development?
- o   maintenance?
- o   production?

3.2.5   For the ten largest applications in the software inventory for the current (base) year of the plan, do records show the expenditures for

- o   development?
- o   maintenance?
- o   production?

3.2.6   For the ten largest applications in the software inventory, do the records show the trends over the past three years for

- o   development?
- o   maintenance?
- o   production?

3.2.7   For each major application in the existing and planned software inventory, is there a projection over the life of the plan that contains an estimate of the

- o   development costs?
- o   maintenance costs?
- o   production costs?
- o   redesign costs?
- o   conversion costs?

3.3   Require Life Cycle Projections for the Hardware Configuration

The key factors and the information base that support management's decisions on the life cycle of a computer configuration should be visible. The decisions should include the planned useful life of (a) each hardware component in the configuration, and (b) operating system software.

3.3.1   Is there a three-year history of the workload processed by the existing hardware configuration (such as in utilization reports)?

    3.3.1.1   Does that history show the hardware configuration use ratio or some similar measurement of hardware use for specific periods for each of the three years?

$$\frac{\text{Actual capacity used}}{\text{Available capacity}} = \text{Hardware configuration use ratio}$$

    3.3.1.2   Does the history show the annual impact on the use ratio of past hardware configuration changes?

3.3.2   Does the planned life cycle for the hardware configuration include a five-year projection of the hardware components use profile which includes all

o   new acquisitions?
o   modifications?

(This projection should show the estimated annual use of each major comoponent of the hardware configuration.)

    3.3.2.1   Does the planned life cycle for the hardware

include at least a five-year projection of the hardware configuration use ratio? (That is, a ratio that shows the annual overall configuration capacity expected to be used as a percentage of the estimated available capacity.)

3.4   Standardize the Life Cycle Planning Structure

Consistent use of common planning terms over the life cycle is essential to assure effective communication and full understanding among those who contribute to, or are affected by, the systems plan.

3.4.1   Do the planning instructions (or the plan itself) contain a set of standard points (milestones) at which management is scheduled to review, evaluate and make decisions over the life cycle of each

o   major hardware component?
o   software application?

3.4.1.1   Is there a preliminary system plan milestone where (based on a rough plan and broad cost estimates) management is scheduled to make a decision on continuation of the project?

3.4.1.2   Is there a feasibility study milestone where (based on a written report of economic, technical and operational feasibility) management is scheduled to make a decision on continuation or modification of the project.

3.4.1.3   Is there a cost benefit assessment milestone?

3.4.1.4   Is there a system design milestone?

3.4.1.5   Is there a set of system operations milestones?

3.5   Test the Transition from Functional to Technical Specifications

Loss of information during the translation of operational requirements, contained in functional specifications, to working technical design specifications can result in deficient output products. Tests and evaluations to assess consistency should be required. This consistency should include a visible track of records or documents which contain the linkage between each of the different interpretations of the original requirements.

3.5.1   Has a procedure been established by which management can be assured of consistency between functional requirements and technical design specifications?

> 3.5.1.1   Does this procedure require that benchmark testing and evaluation criteria for every major hardware component and software application be included as part of the approval of functional specifications?

> 3.5.1.2   Is the participation and understanding of the intended major users required for development of the benchmark tests?

> 3.5.1.3   Is the senior manager of each major organizational unit that will receive support from a planned application required to formalize his concurrence with the benchmark performance criteria?

3.5.2   Does the procedure require that each user provide advance drafts of the different outputs expected when the planned application is completed?

3.5.2.1   Are these sample "draft" outputs or screens prepared, or concurred in, by the person in the functional organization who is expected to use them when the planned systems are in operation?

3.5.2.2   Is the person who will receive and use the output from the completed systems required to acknowledge accountability for assessing whether or not the products satisfy functional specifications?

3.5.2.3   Is this responsibility and accountability formalized by signatures?

3.5.2.4   Where the output is some form of a generalized computational or information retrieval capability, is there a description of these uses under the concurring signature of each person in the organization for whom they are intended?

3.5.3   Has a knowledgeable separate party, not involved in the statement of systems requirements, evaluated the benchmark criteria against the expectations in the functional specifications and assessed the consistency between them?

3.5.3.1   Was the internal auditor used for this task?

3.5.4   Where there is no audit trail of the above consistency (between stated requirements and preliminary technical design) is there a written statement from one or more managers of major functional organizational units which identifies the reasons the trail is missing?

3.5.4.1   Are such statements identified as the source of investment risks and brought to the attention of top management as part of the review of the long-range IS plan?

3.5.4.2   Has a preliminary or tentative design, which has not been previously accomplished anywhere else and for which there is no existing precedent, been identified as a resource investment risk?

3.6   Require Compliance with Standards

For reasons of economy, compatibility and intraorganizational unit communication, technical and operational standards should be formalized and published.

3.6.1   Do planning instructions require compliance with some set of IS standards?

3.6.1.1   Are the technical standards generally comparable with those outlined in the publications of national bodies such as the American National Standards Institute or the National Bureau of Standards? (There should be some reference to these publications.)

3.6.1.2   If not, are comparable standards in force?

3.6.1.3   Is there an additional set of technical specifications used to improve communications and compatibility of systems within the company?

3.6.1.4   Is there a minimum set of functional specifications which must be included in all requirements?

3.7   Establish a Planning Time Frame

The time frame for achieving long-range systems objectives should be identified.   Typically, the minimum period covered should be five years.

3.7.1   Has a time frame been set within which long-range systems objectives are to be achieved?

3.7.2   Is that time frame at least five years?

3.7.3   Is that time frame consistent with the long-range company objectives which the IS plan is supporting?

3.8   Maintain Planning Policies and Procedures Up-to-Date

Responsibility and accountability for maintaining the written planning regulations, instructions and guidelines up-to-date should be assigned to a senior headquarters staff member.

3.8.1   Is there documentation which assigns responsibility for maintaining the written planning regulations, instructions, and guidelines up-to-date?

3.8.1.1   Is this responsibility assigned to a senior member of the headquarters staff?

3.9   Require a List of Long-Range Objectives

The heads of all organizational units that receive a prescribed level of systems support annually should be required to list their long-range IS objectives. The threshold should be set by top management.

3.9.1   Has each unit manager been required to include in his long-range IS plan a ranking of applications by degrees of efficiency, effectiveness, economy of operations and payoff?

3.9.1.1   Are unsatisfactory or marginal support capabilities identified in quantitative terms?

3.9.2   Is each functional manager required to identify existing applications whose modification or enhancement would increase the efficiency, economy or effectiveness of operations?

3.9.2.1   Is there a requirement to describe these modifications or enhancements in quantitative terms?

3.9.3   Is there a requirement that functional managers identify new IS capabilities that will increase the effectiveness of their operations?

3.9.3.1   Are these new requirements identified in quantitative terms?

3.10   Include Planning Assumptions

The objectives of the IS resource investment as a function of company objectives are often changed by events external to the compnay. Political, economic, technical and social trends should be assessed for their impact on the systems plan. For example, new legislation may increase or decrease the projected workload. The head of each organizational unit should make such assessments, and these should be included as assumptions influencing long-range systems objectives.

3.10.1   Is there documentation that shows that the head of each organizational unit does assess trends for impact on his unit's functional tasks in the following areas

o   political?

o   economic?

o   technical?

o   social?

3.10.1.1   Based on the type of assessment mentioned, are factors or assumptions developed which influence the content of long-range IS plans?

3.10.2   Are assumptions included as an integral part of the long-range IS plan?

3.10.2.1   Is there any evidence that the chief executive reviewed the IS planning assumptions and approved them?

3.11   Amplify the IS Objectives

While maintaining consistency in goal direction, objectives should be amplified, documented and used as the basis for project planning.

3.11.1   Is there an objective documented for each application listed in the software inventory?

3.11.2   Can sub-objectives for applications be correlated with the long-range objectives contained in the systems plan?

3.11.3   Is there an audit trail showing consistency of content between the sub-objectives of the applications and the objectives contained in the systems plan?

3.11.4   Do project plans correlate with application objectives?

3.11.5   Are project plans, as a whole, consistent with the long-range objectives? (The project plan is that schedule or estimate of work that is needed to develop a system.)

3.12   Expose Support Problems

Require from the head of each organizational unit a list and description of each existing application which is providing unsatisfactory support or marginal payoff.

3.12.1   Has each functional manager been required to include in his long-range IS plan a list of those applications which he uses but which provide unsatisfactory support or which have only a marginal payoff to his efficiency, effectiveness and economy of operation?

           3.12.1.1   Are the unsatisfactory or marginal support capabilities identified in quantitative terms?

3.12.2   Are the reasons for dissatisfaction documented?

3.13   Exploit New Opportunities

Require from the head of each organizational unit a list and description of new opportunities for use of systems resources which have a potential for enhancing the quality of that unit's or the company's performance.

3.13.1   Is there a requirement that functional managers identify new IS capabilities that will increase the effectiveness of their operations?

           3.13.1.1   Are these new requirements for support identified in quantitative terms?

3.14   Identify the Potential for External Support

Require from the head of each organizational unit a listing and individual description, including estimated cost, of systems support which in his view may usefully be provided by an external source.

3.14.1   Has the head of each organizational unit prepared a list of applications available from an external source that would result in increased productivity or have some other "payoff" if acquired?

        3.14.1.1   For each proposed external support application, is there a requirement that the estimated cost be included?

3.15   Perform an Economic Analysis

A thorough economic analysis allows management to choose one proposed system over other alternatives based on projected costs and benefits. This can only be accomplished when estimates for systems costs and benefits are stated in comparable quantitative terms.

3.15.1   Is there a policy and guidance for the performance of an economic analysis?

3.15.2   Do the guidelines require

        3.15.2.1   investigation of alternatives?

        3.15.2.2   costs and benefits for each alternative?

        3.15.2.3   determination of the relative benefits of each alternative through a comparison of costs and benefits?

        3.15.2.4   a check to validate costs?

        3.15.2.5   documentation of

                o   methodology?

o   source of costs?

o   rationale?

o   assumptions?

o   constraints?

o   priorities?

3.15.2.6   determination and validation of the degree of risk or uncertainty in the results?

3.16   Require a Risk Assessment

Top management should require that a level of investment risk be assessed for each new system or major revision planned. This assessment should include risk factors for software applications, operating system software and hardware as well as overall probability of success or failure. (One useful rule is that the probability of achieving that payoff is directly related to the degree with which the expected performance criteria of a system are quantified.)

3.16.1   Has top management been provided with some assessment of the risks associated with major changes or new system developments?

3.17   Provide for Plan Implementation

The transition from plan to action normally begins with the allocation of funds as part of an approved budget. At this point an official should be designated as responsible and accountable for these resources.

3.17.1   Is there a written document which identifies and holds responsible and accountable a specific official or officials for plan implementation?

3.17.2   Does that document or a separate one allocate or transfer funds or other resources for that purpose to the official(s) identified?

4. CONTROL

Because planning and control are inseparable, the control methods should be an integral part of the planning documents.   While highly dependent on individual management styles, there are, nonetheless, minimum essential elements of management control for systems planning.   The most important of these elements are quantitative performance capabilities. Quantitative terms make it easier to focus on the progress toward achievement of the goals and objectives contained in the systems plan and the business objectives that the systems plan supports.   A visible, easy to understand, quantitative control method also assures effective communication and enhances the organization's commitment to the goals management has set.   The essential elelments of a quantitative method for managing systems planning are presented in this section.   The more specific reporting information needed to maintain the control focus is covered in section 5.

4.1   State All Performance Criteria

A meaningful statement of the results expected when objectives are achieved should be included in the strategy for accomplishment.

4.1.1   Is there a description of the results expected if the objectives are met?

4.1.2   Is the description in quantitative terms?

4.2   Require that Performance Criteria be Quantified.

In each set of expected performance criteria, i.e., for each objective, a quantitative change should be included which can be compared to existing performance to measure progress. If a new or revised capability is being described, it should contain some quantitative information which can be used as a basis for assessing the "payoff" of the investment.

4.2.1 For each objective in the IS plan, is there an accompanying statement of the performance criteria expected when the objective is achieved?

4.2.2 Where such performance criteria are not included with the objectives, is there some other basis in the planning documentation which communicates how achievement of the objective will be recognized?

4.2.3 Are the performance criteria which describe how the achievement of objectives will be recognized presented in quantitative terms?

4.2.4 Can existing performance criteria be compared with expected capabilities stated in project plans to identify differences between present and planned capabilities?

4.2.4.1 Has the central planning staff focused on those differences as a means of identifying what the planned investment in IS resources will buy?

4.2.4.2 Has the central planning staff reviewed the impact of proposed projects in IS capabilities and reported in writing its assessment and recommendations?

4.3 Quantify User Requirements

Descriptions of functional user requirements should be stated in terms that show a quantitative difference between existing manual or automated capabilities and those that are needed.

4.3.1 Is the existing system, or capability, described in quantitative terms?

4.3.2   Are the different organizational units that receive support from the existing capability identified?

4.3.3   Is the support received by each of these organizational units described in quantitative or other terms that provide an understanding of its impact on the operations of the units?

4.3.4   Are new requirements described in terms that show a quantitative difference between existing capabilities and those proposed?

4.3.5   Do those organizational units that will be supported by the requirements for new or revised capabilities agree with the need expressed?

4.3.6   Were all of the requirements for new or revised capabilities written by the organizational units that will be supported by those systems?

4.4   Quantify Expected Benefits

If the expected capabilities required by a new system, i.e., a software application, a hardware configuration or a mix of both added to an existing system, are achieved, the results should reflect identifiable benefits. Such benefits should be documented in terms that permit top management to assess the value to the organization of the investment.

4.4.1   Is there a cost benefit study or similar document which describes the benefits of the system?

4.4.2   Are quantitative performance capabilities in the cost benefit study described for individual applications? (By "quantitative" we exclude words like improved, better, faster, etc. We include numbers that can be compared with other numbers.)

4.4.4.2   If the answer is "no," what percentage of the existing inventory of application programs has its performance capabilities described in quantitative terms?

4.5   Quantify Existing Software Assets

Computer programs should be described in simple, consistent, realistic quantitative terms that are understandable to all levels of the organization. Two such criteria might include (1) the total number of instructions or lines of code per application, and (2) the average cost per instruction.

4.5.1   Is there an inventory of all the software assets?

4.5.1.1   Is the software inventory accounted for in a manner comparable to other capital assets?

4.5.2   Was an overview of the software inventory presented to top management as part of the IS plan?

4.5.2.1   Does the overview identify the programs in use, the users, the total cost, the number of different languages and other relevant items from the software inventory?

4.5.3   Was an overview of the file inventory presented to top management as part of the IS plan?

4.5.3.1   Does the overview identify the files, the users whose requirements generated the input to each file, the size and cost of the file, growth trends and other relevant information?

4.6   Require that Proposed New or Revised Applications Be Quantified

Unless some other basis is used to indicate the size of software applications, the estimated total number of lines of code per application and
the estimated cost per line should be included in the plan.

4.6.1   Are the number of lines of code and the cost per line for each
          proposed new or revised application estimated?

          4.6.1.1   If estimates are not included, is there some other
                      reasonable method of quantifying the projections
                      for new or improved software?

          4.6.1.2   Is this other method consistent with the way
                      software assets are quantified and valued for the
                      organization?

          4.6.1.3   Where there is no method for quantifying pro-
                      jected software applications, does the plan
                      contain a reasonable method for estimating the
                      cost and size of the software applications?

4.6.2   When planned applications are examined side-by-side with the
          existing software inventory, is there a year-to-year visible
          change in the size and value of the inventory?

          4.6.2.1   If the change is one of growth, can that growth
                      be correlated with increased or new capabilities?

          4.6.2.2   If there is no growth in the size of the inventory,
                      but there is still an increase in capabilities, can
                      that increase be attributed to enhanced product-
                      ivity?

4.7   Quantify Existing Hardware Capability

All components of the hardware configuration should be recorded in an asset inventory so that the total capital investment and other asset accounting information can be maintained up to date.

4.7.1   Are hardware acquisitions proposed in the plan justified on the basis of system capacity?

        4.7.1.1   Have performance monitors been used in these analyses?

        4.7.1.2   Is there a historical record of the system accounting data which was used in this analysis?

4.7.2   Is there a historical record (at least three years) which shows the difference between system capacity available and that actually used?

4.7.3   Is the annual size of the expected overage or shortage in system capacity estimated for the life of the plan?

        4.7.3.1   Are the alternative approaches that were analyzed to plan the operating capacity shown?

4.7.4   Are the studies of capacity overages or shortages presented in capability performance terms as well as system capacity terms? (That is, in terms that can be correlated directly with the operational performance requirements of those who use the system output.)

4.8   Require that Proposed Hardware Acquisitions Be Quantified

All costs for planned hardware should be estimated and aggregated in the same quantitative terms used for the existing hardware inventory.

4.8.1   Has the proposed hardware inventory been analyzed and a profile developed as to who will use it?

      4.8.1.1   Does this aggregation identify the cost of each major user's output as a percentage of the proposed system cost?

4.8.2   Is each user required to acknowledge, in writing, the percentage so attributed?

4.9   Quantify Existing System Products

To provide a basis for correlating aggregate costs with specific types of operations (such as for application programs, maintenance or development) the output for the entire system should be identified. This identification should be in easily understood terms, such as the number of lines of print, number of pages or other acceptable units of ouput.

4.9.1   Is there an estimate of the total cost of each distinct output product produced by the current IS operation?

      4.9.1.1   Can the output products of each application be totalled to indicate the cost of all products of that system?

      4.9.1.2   Can these output products be identified so that the overall cost of the application can be traced to one or a group of end users who receive the output products?

4.9.2   What percentage of the total current operation is costed as described above?

4.10   Require that Proposed Outputs Be Quantified

Itemize and describe the products expected of planned systems. These products can then be compared with those of the existing manual or automated procedure being replaced, and the reasons for the investment made visible in quantitative terms.

4.10.1　Is there an inventory of the output reports or screens expected from each computer application contained in the plan?

4.10.1.1　Does this inventory show the expected user of each such product?

4.10.1.2　Is there an estimated cost shown for each type of output in the proposed output inventory?

4.10.1.3　Does each recipient of the output receive the estimated cost of that planned output?

4.10.2　Does a comparison of the current and planned output inventories show the magnitude of planned changes in terms of the existing output?

4.10.3　Can the planned output inventory be correlated with user requirements to pinpoint management accountability?

4.10.4　Does the record show that the central planning staff examined the current and planned output inventories as part of their review?

4.10.5　Does the record show that the steering committee reviewed and approved the existing and planned output inventories?

4.11　Require that Development Risk Be Quantified

Research and development investments and any investment for which planned products are not quantified should have a confidence level assigned and be supported by a narrative describing the risks.

4.11.1   Are there any existing or planned computer applications, or systems, that have not been quantified as described above?

4.11.1.1   Has a confidence level, identifying the risk, been established?

4.11.1.2   Is there a narrative explanation of the risk which includes the position of the sponsor of the effort?

4.11.2   Are these risk areas reviewed by the central planning staff?

4.11.3   Were the risk areas reviewed and approved by the steering committee?

5. REPORTING

The reporting system for IS resource usage should be in the mainstream of information used by management to control all its resources. The feedback should be described in terms that show the link to accomplishments projected in the plan. It should report actual against planned performance in such key areas as (a) the software that controls and coordinates the computer system (system software), (b) user specific application software that performs mission-related functions, (c) hardware components and (d) total dollar resources used by accountable management. The use of quantitative criteria as the basis for this type of control information was emphasized in the previous section.

In this section some types of reports that can assist management to detect deviations from planned accomplishments are described. Because most are quantitative, a graph or table reporting format could be devised. Such reports are essential for the control of plan implementation.

5.1   Require Organization-wide IS Resources Accounting and Control

The senior financial officer should be held responsible for providing an organization-wide system of IS resource accounting and control. This system should regularly provide top management with a current record of all IS resources, visibility as to their status, use, use trends, costs, cost trends and other analyses needed for developing plan starting points, projections and plan progress. It should provide similar feedback to the head of each organizational unit that uses IS support.

5.1.1   Is the senior financial officer required to maintain an organization-wide accounting of IS resources?

5.1.2   Is the senior financial officer required to provide accounting information that can be used for planning and control of IS resource investments and expenses to the

o   chief executive?
o   functional managers?

   5.1.2.1   Is information provided on capital investments in

      o   computer hardware?
      o   new software (both applications and operating systems)?
      o   major conversions of existing software?
      o   major upgrades of existing software?

5.1.3   Does the accounting system maintain records in a form that permits the output of each application to be quantified?

   5.1.3.1   Can the accounting system provide information needed to compute the cost per item of output for an application?

   5.1.3.2   Does the quantitative information maintained by the accounting system provide a data base which can be used to assist in determining whether forecasted results and estimated costs have been achieved?

5.1.4   Is the manager of each organizational unit routinely charged for all computer services received or otherwise routinely made aware of the cost of services received?

5.1.5   Is the manager of each organizational unit required to prepare a budget for the anticipated costs of computer services?

5.2   Provide Life Cycle Costing

The accounting system should provide cumulative sums of actual costs for the life cycle of each major application in the software inventory and the major components of the hardware system.

5.2.1   Are costs accumulated over the life cycle of each application?

5.2.2   Can the accounting system provide cost accumulation for a single phase (or a single year) within the life cycle of an application?

5.2.3   Can the accounting system provide comparisons between cost estimates and actual costs for each phase (year) of the life cycle of an application?

5.2.4   Are the actual IS resource costs of each major organizational unit itemized and reported to the heads of those units on a routine basis?

5.2.5   Are the costs of interdepartmental applications accumulated and aggregated across all departments to identify the full cost of such applications?

5.2.5.1   Are the life cycle costs of interdepartmental applications available in the financial records?

5.2.6   Can the accounting system be used by all levels of management to flag excessive costs for a life cycle phase (or some similar event) in time to take corrective action and preclude unanticipated resource expenditures?

5.3   Require Reports on Implementation of the IS Plan

There should be a formalized reporting system that provides to top management, on a regular basis, information as to problems, opportunities and deviations between planned and actual performance.

5.3.1   Is there an adminstrative procedure in use that extracts and relates the projected performance criteria contained in the plan to tangible objectives against which progress can be compared?

5.3.1.1   Is this information used as a basis for reporting progress toward its achievement?

5.3.1.2   Is this done for computer resources actually used in some accepted standard unit? For example, is central processing unit (CPU) time actually used reported and compared with performance objectives for CPU use contained in the plan?

5.3.1.3   Is it done for revision of existing application programs? For example, are the revisions planned for application programs translated into tangible performance goals for specific users?

5.3.1.4   Is it done for design and use of new application

programs? For example, are the expected performance criteria for new applications translated into tangible performance goals for specific users?

5.3.1.5   Is it done for all major objectives established in the plan? For example, are all major objectives in the plan similarly translated into tangible performance goals for specific users?

5.3.1.6   Does the status information contained in progress reports focus on tangible performance goals such as those described above?

5.4   Require a Software Inventory Report

The chief executive should have a feel for the scope, composition, complexity and status of the total application portfolio. This report is as important as the inventory records for any major corporate asset.

5.4.1   Is there an inventory of software applications?

5.4.1.1   Is the inventory updated on at least an annual basis?

5.4.2   If a decision were made to upgrade or otherwise improve an application, would the software inventory contain enough technical, operational and cost detail to be usable in the development of new specifications?

5.4.3   Is there an inventory of the files?

5.4.3.1   Is the inventory updated on at least an annual basis?

5.4.4   If a decision were made to upgrade, or otherwise modify an application, would the file inventory contain enough technical, operational and cost information to be usable in the development of new specifications?

5.5   Require a Hardware Inventory Report

Top management should have available a hardware inventory report which lists each different hardware component, its cost, the manufacturer, its age, its reliability and other relevant factors. The report should be formated in such a manner as to highlight (1) the cumulative changes from the previous year's report and (2) any trends in the composition and overall value of the inventory.

5.5.1   Is there an inventory of all computer and communications equipment, both purchased and leased, including small computers and terminals?

   5.5.1.1   Is it kept up-to-date on at least an annual basis?

   5.5.1.2   Does it show changes from the previous year?

   5.5.1.3   Does it show changes projected for the next year?

   5.5.1.4   Does it show the age of each component?

   5.5.1.5   Does it show the system software supplied with the hardware?

   5.5.1.6   Does it contain figures that indicate the costs of the various components?

   5.5.1.7   Does it contain one figure showing the total cost of the inventory that is actually on board?

(NOTE: This is not the depreciated value.)

5.5.2   Does the chief executive indicate by signature or initials on the report that the inventory report is seen at least once a year?

5.6   Require Auditor Review and Report on Plans

The internal audit staff should review the system planning structure, and the completed plan, and provide an evaluation report to the chief executive. This report should present an assessment of the degree to which plans support company policies and objectives.

5.9.1   Are the internal auditors required to review and validate any portion of the systems plan on a regular basis?

5.9.2   Are the reports of such audits available?

5.9.3   Does top management review these audit reports prior to making decisions on the content of the long-range IS plan?

5.9.4   Does top management have some other methods for assuring that the estimates for IS support are reasonable and based on factual information.

5.9.5   Does the audit report advise top management whether the projected systems support is directly or indirectly supportive of specific company policies and objectives?

Index

Ackoff, Russell L., 96

airline systems, 4-5, 19-20, 41, 56, 88

Anthony, Robert N., 20-21

application inventory, see software inventory

banking systems, 19-20, 25, 33-34, 41, 56

BASIC programming language, 105

benefits of planning, 34-36

Blumenthal, Sherman C., 19

bottom-up planning, 11, 35, 46-48, 101

budgeting, 33, 49-51, 62-63, 106-107, 113, 121

business planning, see corporate planning

business systems planning (BSP), 72

capacity planning, 12-13, 91-93

charging back, 36, 50-51, 53, 85, 91

COBOL programming language, 65, 67, 105

competitive practices, 17-20, 48, 121

consultants, use of, 76-77

contingency planning, 28, 106, 120

contract programming, 49, 65, 85

controls, 104-111

conversion planning, 64-67

corporate planning, 3-4, 10-11, 14, 45-49, 59, 63-64, 76, 103, 120

costs, 53, 85-87, 107

critical path method, 12

cross impact analysis, 96-97

data collection, 77-87

decentralization, 16, 53-55, 63-64, 74, 77, 89, 101, 103-104, 110

delphi forecasting technique, 95
deterrents to planning, 101-104
distributed processing, 16, 42, 91

Emery, James C., 27
envelope curves, 94
environmental considerations, 17-18
episodic planning, 96, 98
equipment inventory, 77-79, 120

factory automation, 42
feasibility studies, 34, 57, 109
FORTRAN programming language, 67, 105

Gibson, Cyrus F., 39-42, 88
goals, 6-8, 14, 19-21, 59-64, 73-74, 96, 98, 113, 119

hardware inventory, see equipment inventory
Head, Robert V., 23-26, 88

IBM, 15, 72
information resources management, 43-45

length of plan, 113
levels of planning, 6-10, 21-27, 59-63
life cycle management, 12, 56-60, 64, 89-90, 106, 109-110

maintenance of applications, 51-52, 64
management by objectives, 14
management information systems, 23-28, 56, 87-89, 119
McFarlan, F. Warren, 80
minicomputers, 1, 16, 43, 55, 93, 105, 109

Nolan, Richard L., 39-42, 88

objectives, 6-8, 14, 59-62

obsolescence, 15, 64

office automation, 16, 42-43

on-line systems, 1, 33, 65, 89

paperless office, 42

personnel, 18, 71, 78, 84, 107, 110-111, 121

PERT, see program evaluation and review technique

planning task forces, 72-75

policy considerations, 19-20, 45-49, 72

procedures for planning, 8-10, 34, 72, 77, 103, 119

procurement, 94, 107-109

program evaluation and review technique, 12, 106

programmed decision making, 26-27, 88

prior approvals, 109-111

project management, see life cycle management

project planning, 12, 51-64, 91, 109-110, 113

project selection, 35, 51-55, 64-67, 91

projections, 75, 91-95, 120

requirements analysis, 75-76, 87-91

risk analysis, 32

sample plans, 111-119

scope of systems planning, 42-43

setting priorities, see project selection

Simon, Herbert A., 26-27, 88

simulation, 96

Society for Management Information Systems, 33

software inventory, 78, 81, 89-91, 120

software packages, 49, 105

staff written plans, 75-76

stages of growth, 39-42, 88

standards, 104-106

steering committees, see systems steering committees

structured programming, 12, 107

suboptimization, 55, 74

systems steering committees, 34, 48, 51-53, 59

tactical planning, 4

technological forecasting, see technology assessment

technology assessment, 13, 15-17, 45, 93-96, 120-121

top-down planning, 35, 45-48

transaction processing, 25, 33, 56, 65

uncertainty in planning, 16-17. 27-32

U.S. Department of Agriculture, 33

U.S. Department of Defense, 56

U.S. General Services Administration, 108

U.S. Internal Revenue Service, 56

U.S. National Bureau of Standards, 57

U.S. Social Security Administration, 56

word processing, 42-43

zero base budgeting, 50